ALSO BY CHERISA JEREZ

For Those Left Behind

Broken & Redeemed

941-807-2570

Irene Lieberman

To Pastor

CONQUERED

The story of one clinic's journey from death to life

Genesis 50-20

A story told by

JEANNE M. PERNIA

&

And written by

Cherisa Jerez

First published 2013

ISBN-13:978-1492148081
ISBN-10:1492148083

Printed in the United States of America

This book is printed on acid-free paper.

Cover image provided by Heartbeat of Miami Pregnancy Help Medical Clinic

Scripture quotations are taken from the Holy Bible, New Living Translation, copyright 1996. Used by permission of Tyndale House Publishers, Inc., Wheaton, IL 60189. All rights reserved.

Cover design by Alberto M. Jerez

*This book is dedicated to my grandmother,
Irene Liberman.
May your legacy of strong women setting out to
make a difference live on for many generations
to come.*

Author's Note

I am deeply blessed to be able to put the story of my family's legacy down on paper. I genuinely struggled with whether or not I was to be the writer of this story, but in the end it wasn't my decision, it was the Lord's. He pressed upon my heart that not only was I selected to write this, but he would ensure it would all come together quickly. And by His grace, it has.

I didn't have an intended "voice" when I began to write. I reviewed all of my mother's notes, her emails, and even her own private writings of all these events and somehow, as I began to put her story on paper, the natural first person account of what happened revealed itself.

I'm sure it wasn't easy for her to read my "version" of her memories, but I made sure to have her review the first, fifth, and final drafts of each chapter to ensure the integrity of the story.

I won't say I didn't take a little bit of creative freedom. I am a writer, after all. But the facts listed in each chapter are exactly that – facts. There were no embellishments added in order to make the story more interesting. All of the accounts are true and factual to the best of my mother's ability to remember. Although I've found that her memory of these events are ingrained so deeply in her heart she can still recall the events as though they were yesterday.

My prayers are that the tragedy, the healing, and the redemption of this family legacy is a blessing to all who read it. We that serve Christ are *...more than conquerors through him who loved us. [38] For I am convinced that neither death nor life, neither angels nor demons,[b] neither the present nor the future, nor any powers, [39] neither height nor depth, nor anything else in all creation, will be able to separate us from the love of God that is in Christ Jesus our Lord.*

Romans 8:37-39

- Cherisa Jerez

A Note from Jeanne M. Pernia

I have been trying to find the right format to tell my story for several years now. I wanted to share the truth behind the entire testimony. I now understand why it has taken a bit longer than I originally expected, as the story was not yet complete. It had not gone full circle until this year.

This is it. This is the story of the place where my first child was killed. The same place where today I have helped thousands of other women choose life. This story shares how God can bring right from wrong and life from death.

Today, I am excited to share that I was able to conceive three beautiful children after my abortion and my eldest daughter has not only brought joy to my life but also life to this story. Through her literary skills, she has been able to capture the reality of my memories and the emotion I've felt at each stage of my life. She has written this story for me like no one else could have.

I am so very grateful to God for blessing me with family, friends, and the leaders, specifically Reverend John Ensor, who have given me direction, discipleship and above all unconditional love. My daughter has dedicated this book to my mother and it is my prayer that she is proud of what the Lord has done.

CONQUERED

The story of one clinic's journey from death to life

Table of Contents

Prologue – At Death's Door
Irene

xix

Chapter One – Seeds of Redemption
Jeanne

1

Chapter Two – Beginning the Cycle of Death in Miami
Jeanne & Irene

11

Chapter Three – All Roads Lead to Hialeah
Hialeah

19

Chapter Four – A Business Venture
The Clinic

25

Chapter Five – There Was No Denying
The Women

31

Chapter Six – A Personal Connection
Jeanne's Story

41

Chapter Seven – Ending the Legacy
Irene's Story

49

Chapter Eight – Moving on to a New Life
Jeanne's Story Part II

53

Chapter Nine – A Walk through the Desert
Jeanne's Story Part III

65

Chapter Ten – The Redemption Promise
From Death to Life

71

Chapter Eleven – It All Comes Full Circle
More than Conquerors

85

Epilogue – The Statistics
The Fight for Life

97

Acknowledgments

101

Sources

103

PROLOGUE

At Death's Door
IRENE

December 1981

The fluorescent blue lights above the operating table cast a sallow green tone to the naturally bronzed skin of the Native American woman whose shallow breaths filled the tense room with sound. Sweat formulated into small beads at the top of her hair line. The room was cold and sterile, but she was still sweating. It didn't make sense, but her sweat was the last of anyone's concerns.

There was an ambulance en route. Irene looked at the young woman lying on the table as she paced back and forth near the exit. The patient remained eerily still.

Thank God she's still alive, she thought to herself. It was only by a miracle, and possibly the antibiotic she'd just injected into the young woman's vein, but she was still alive.

The two doctors who should have been attending her were instead shouting at each other somewhere in the distance. Irene could faintly trace the scent of a cigarette. It wouldn't have surprised her in the least that he would light a cigarette at a time like this.

This was wrong, this was all wrong. He was a physician. He wasn't supposed to make these types of mistakes. And yet somehow he had, and now a woman's life hung in the balance.

Irene prayed that ambulance would get there quickly. She didn't have much time. That much she was sure of.

The patient's hand moved absently to her rounded belly. She was murmuring. The medication was wearing off. They didn't have much time.

Time was moving so slowly. Nothing felt real. This had to be some kind of nightmare. On instinct, Irene approached the table and stroked the woman's forehead. "Sssshh. Ssssshh. It's okay. Everything's going to be ok."

The patient's eyes did not open, but her hand remained poised atop her abdomen.

Unable to wait any longer, Irene opened the door to the surgical room and peered out toward the hallway. The faint sound of sirens grew louder in the distance.

They're coming.

She could hear the two doctors shouting in her office. They were arguing about what to do. This wasn't supposed to happen. One kept screaming that he wasn't going to get arrested. He wasn't going to jail for this. The other doctor, Irene's husband, kept shouting for him to calm down. Everything was going to be okay.

But she knew that was a lie. They had nearly killed someone. If it wasn't for her intervention, they most likely would have intentionally murdered an innocent woman. As far as the doctors were concerned, killing her would have been much easier than allowing her to live. If she lived, there was likely to be an investigation. But that was going way too far. Irene would not stand for murder in her clinic. Which could have been considered an oxymoron considering her clinic was established to conduct abortions, but she was not going to allow her husband to kill an innocent woman. Instead she opted at the most critical moment to step in and intervene. She gave the patient the antibiotics and kept her alive. As far as the law was concerned she should be a hero. She saved a woman's life. Not only that, but it was likely she'd saved the baby as well.

They'd had no idea how far along she really was when they scheduled her for the procedure. The baby was breach. Her stomach was small. When they measured her using the tape measure there was no way to tell. The woman was well into her third trimester, but she'd never told them. She'd lied and it was almost too late before they'd discovered the truth. Her baby was nearly delivered. Late term abortions were illegal and now they had a real situation on their hands.

The siren became nearly deafening as the van pulled up into the parking lot. The ambulance was here. There was a loud knock on the front door. She listened as one of the doctors exited the building through the back door. There was no doubt. If this woman was going to live, Irene would have to be the one to save her.

Making the only decision she deemed possible, Irene ran to the front door and let the EMT crew in.

"Please, follow me," she urged. "She went into labor. We didn't know. We simply didn't know."

The response team moved quickly to move the woman's body onto the gurney. She was becoming more and more coherent and began crying and howling in pain.

Irene closed her eyes as the crew pushed past her and placed the woman in the back of the ambulance.

She took a deep breath, attempting to breathe a sigh of relief. It was over. She was safe. As many procedures as she'd seen over the years, she was nearly certain the woman would make it. Her baby might be born premature, but at nearly thirty-two weeks, the likelihood was high that the baby would, too, survive.

For a split second, amidst the silence everything seemed quiet and back under control. It took a minute to understand why her husband had rushed passed her and slammed the front door shut.

She was gone. The patient was gone. What was the problem?

It was then that Irene saw through the glass of the front windows the blue and white lights of the parked police car and the large antennae of the news van that was parked beside it.

CHAPTER ONE

Seeds of Redemption
Jeannie

October 1974

"I want you to reach your hand here. Can you feel her cervix? Can you tell if her cervix is closed?"

I stared at the young Indian doctor with worry-filled blue eyes. She wanted me to reach my hand inside this woman? How was I supposed to know if the cervix was closed? I wasn't even sure I knew exactly what a cervix was.

"Don't be shy, child. The only way to learn medicine is to *do*, not to read. You must *do*. Now this woman is twenty-four weeks along. Give me your hand."

Thankfully her patient had been forewarned prior to the examination that the doctor wanted to use her visit as an opportunity to teach and mentor her young new medical assistant in training.

And I was definitely young, only sixteen years old. When most of my peers were trying to land part-time jobs at the local movie theater, I was diligently spending all of my after school hours learning the day to day processes and routine examinations related to obstetrics and gynecology.

My mentor was a young and beautiful doctor from India. She was kind and endlessly dedicated to her patients and her employees. She even tried to convince my mother to allow me to move to India after high school, where she assured her I would get a world class education in the field of medicine.

"Your daughter is a natural," she would say. "She was born to do this. She has the gift of delivering babies."

If only she knew how her prophetic words would twist and shape my life.

***

January 2005

A typical spring morning in the beautiful town of Miami Lakes, FL portrays a renewal of life and refreshment for the soul. It's a cascade of lavender hibiscus and pompano pink plumeria flowers, warm and moist morning breezes, and dewy grass expanses. It's a small tropical paradise nestled quietly to the left of the surrounding concrete suburbs of Hialeah, Opa-Locka, and Miami Gardens. Miami Gardens is more aptly described as endless streets of metal warehouses and a lack of vegetation, not much of a garden at all.

Miami Lakes is different. It's a costly but untouched city. It allows its residents to avoid the over industrialization and commercialization of the surrounding areas; opting instead, to remain a prestigiously well-designed tropical, yet residential paradise. This, in turn, leaves its residents somewhat less affected by the overpopulation of South Florida over the last fifty years. Instead these residents boast beautifully manicured lawns and updated homes nearly all renovated to their original beauty. This assures the ability to maintain property values and an unchanged quality of life.

In Miami Lakes quaint boutiques and French cafés meld together with contemporary restaurants and an updated movie theater for the occasional tourist or native patron to revel in without having to make the twenty-five minute drive to one of the local popular beach spots. This is the quaint town I returned to after a sixteen year crossing of my own desert in far west Texas. Yes, it had been a long road, but I had finally circled the walls and entered into the land of milk and honey, complete with a predestined schoolhouse down the street.

My days of needing a schoolhouse were long since over as my three children were now grown with children of their own, but there was more to this place than I'd originally thought. The school district allowed the building to host a local church on Sunday mornings. This particular congregation used the school stage in the center of an auditorium as a pulpit and the actual auditorium as a worship sanctuary. Its classrooms served as Sunday school classrooms for the children. Even more ideal, and clearly part of a divinely designed plan, was its placement, only a short distance from the condominium my husband and I had just rented in my newfound paradise.

I found myself one Sunday morning walking in through the large metal doors, passing the rows of grey metal lockers on either side of the hallway as I made my way to the auditorium. I was a bit puzzled by the choice of location for a church, but as I stepped inside, the small room filled with the beginning staccato of a small worship band. I knew I was exactly where I was called to be. The Lord immediately gave me the all too familiar affirmation within my heart, assuring me I'd found my church home. And like all gardens of fruition, this particular morning was only to be the first seed of the next calling in my life - my phase of impending redemption.

April 2006

Only a little after one year of church attendance, the Lord decided that my time to begin the work of the kingdom had begun. I had become close to a fellow Sunday patron. She and I shared a similar cultural background, both being New York City natives of Puerto Rican descent, at least on my mother's side. On my father's side I was a second generation Irish-American. My Irish grandfather had even gone so far as to engrave his name on the famous monument at Ellis Island near the Statue of Liberty as part of a tribute to the legacy he would leave his future generations in their newfound America. This combination of Irish-American and Puerto Rican-American heritage left me to be the product of a tumultuous and racial stirred time period in the blazing borough of the Bronx, New York, something I felt my dear friend at church could relate to. I had no idea this newfound friendship would share another similarity – a mutual travesty.

That particular morning she was called to speak. I wasn't aware of the details so instead I watched as she bravely stepped up to the podium and began to share with an entire congregation of people, the story of her decision to elect an abortion for an unexpected pregnancy. I watched her hands tremble as she held the base of the microphone. I stared down at the trembling of my own hands, matching the fear in hers. Feelings I had quelled beneath an armor of internal resistance threatened to rise back up to the forefront of my mind, a place I had long since banished them from.

How could she possibly stand up there and share something so private and personal with a room filled with so many strangers? This was a church, for goodness sake, a public forum, not exactly the ideal place to make such a profound revelation. How could the audience NOT judge her for a decision so opposed to those who claim to be followers of Christ?

I immediately felt ashamed for my own judgments. As I thought about it, I realized that there was no better place for her to confess her sins than in a room filled with her fellow brothers and sisters. This was her chance to experience the gift of mercy and forgiveness from those who strive to be representatives of the All Merciful.

It was then I realized that it wasn't her I was condemning. It was much more personal than that. As I watched her stand there in the center of the stage, so vulnerable and filled with regret, my own shame reflected back at me. I was in no place emotionally to allow myself grace or forgiveness, so instead I hid behind judgment. It felt more comfortable there. It was judgment, shame, and regret that justified my own actions in forcing away the thoughts of my tragedy and my role in the circumstances of so many others.

I watched her finish her story as I forced the tears that threatened to show themselves back into the corners of my eyes. I could not allow them to reveal the secrets I knew I would never have revealed otherwise.

I debated whether or not I should excuse myself and step quietly away to the ladies room, but reconsidered. That would be too obvious a gesture and would affirm my own culpability. The last thing I wanted was for all eyes to be on me as I stood to rise.

So I sat very, very still and waited for the whole thing to be over.

Then a Reverend stood up and gave my friend a comforting hug, taking her place at the center of the small stage. He was a visiting speaker, the Executive Director of an Urban Initiative in the Pro-Life Ministries. He represented an organization called *Heartbeat International*. They were an organization that wanted to conduct a pilot program in Miami. Research about certain statistics in the area was very troublesome, forcing the city to stand out for reasons that would, most likely, have brought shame to many of the local residents. He had a message for the patrons of Miami and its surrounding areas, to include my own picturesque town of Miami Lakes, where bad things weren't supposed to happen.

Here are just a few of the key statistics he discussed and other relevant data I've since researched about my beloved city.

Abortion Statistics for Florida and Miami-Dade County

1. Florida has consistently been listed among the top five states to conduct the highest number of abortions in the United States yearly.

2. *Forty percent* of all abortions conducted in Florida occur in Miami-Dade County. *Sixty-four percent* of the Miami-Dade area is listed as Hispanic or Latino. *Nineteen point two percent* are listed as Black or African American, making Miami-Dade County an area populated with an *eighty-three point two percent* minority population and the highest termination rate in the state.

3. In the United States, while African American women represent *thirteen percent* of the female population, they undergo *thirty-seven percent* of the abortions. Hispanic women represent *fourteen percent* of the female population and undergo *twenty-two percent* of the abortions. Combined these two minorities represent only *twenty-seven percent* of the female population in the U.S, yet they undergo *fifty-nine percent* of all abortions.

4. In the Miami area there are *thirty-seven* abortion centers, not including local hospitals, for every *one* pregnancy help center, the highest known disparity of any city in the United States. This also represents nearly *forty percent* of the abortion centers in the state of Florida, concentrated in this one particular area.

5. The abortion rate for the United States is *fifteen* abortions per *thousand* women aged 15-44, for Florida its *twenty-seven point two* abortions for every *thousand* women.

These statistics left me nearly sick to my stomach as I shifted uncomfortably in my chair, nervously clearing my throat.

Could this really be happening?

After nearly twenty-six years of silence, I was being confronted, head-on, with the plague of death that I began in this area. Was I responsible for what had become of our city?

I could no longer maintain my resolve and the tears silently poured down my cheeks as I realized my role in the origin of these statistics.

See, this was somewhat my fault. I started it.

My very own mother and her silent partner had once opened up one of the first abortion centers in Hialeah, a small suburb directly to the east of Miami Lakes. We were one of the first to operate in the area back in the early 1970s.

The cycle of death in that town began with me. I was the one who brought her to the area and introduced her to the booming business of abortion. It was in that same building that I, too, underwent the abortion of my first pregnancy causing the center to resonate to a whole other existence in my already shattered life.

As I listened to the Reverend continue to speak, I realized that this just might be my chance to do something to stop it, once and for all.

He was in Miami with a mission. After having successfully opened six pregnancy help clinics in his native town of Boston, he began to research the growing number of abortion facilities across the nation. After careful review of the statistics provided by a well known pro-life organization called CareNet and the data listed publicly under the Center for Disease Control (CDC) website, Miami stood out as a city with a growing epidemic - silently destroying the unborn. He claimed that it was time to unleash the truth about the daily cycles of death going on around us. "It is up to the church," he exclaimed, "to make a difference toward change."

As the church service concluded, I stood with tear stained cheeks and a heavy heart knowing what had to be done. The Holy Spirit pressed heavily within my own spirit as I realized this was my chance to choose obedience. I was being given the chance to take up my cross and follow Jesus. It was time for me to confess my pain, my past, and trust that there was healing and maybe even redemption waiting for me.

CHAPTER TWO

Beginning the Cycle of Death in Miami

Jeannie & **IRENE**

March 1976

Originally born Irene Delgado, my mother was a fiercely motivated, independent, free spirit. Born in New York City, the only child of two Puerto Rican immigrants and raised in the streets of the Bronx, she had a strong will and a desire to sculpt her success via the work of her own two hands and shrewdly sharp mind. She was a woman who refused to let any of life's challenges get in her way and she frequently relied on the beguiling strength of her overt beauty to open doors that would not have opened otherwise. Her parenting style was non-traditional to say the least, and it was perfectly normal to be treated more like her sister than her daughter in my early teenage years. She was not outright interested in the nurturing and responsibility role of mother and caretaker. As far as she was concerned, there was a world to discover and negotiations toward success to be made. She saw greater value in imparting in me a hands-on observational approach toward life. She conquered – I observed, and rather than stand behind her representing the baggage of a needy child, she placed me beside her as a quiet but astute upcoming protégé. Standing side-by-side this force of a woman, I began to validate the lens through which I saw life.

A painful divorce in 1974 from my Cuban stepfather in south Miami was enough of a reason for my mother, now a mother of four (my older brother and I and my two younger siblings) to retreat back to her hometown of New York City. Running from a situation has never been an ideal resolution and as might be expected, she quickly fell back into another dysfunctional relationship in New York, dating a married Cuban man who served as the administrator for a clinic where she worked.

In terms of education she was licensed to work only as a medical assistant, but my mother's wit and shrewd business sense knew no bounds. She had a skill for learning and an accompanying entrepreneurial spirit. The combination of those two qualities, in addition to her newfound romance assured her advancement in the business. Shortly after starting work with a small clinic in Harlem, she was running the entire operation.

In the seventies there was still much to be desired in terms of quality control when dealing with the Medicaid/Medicare system. Small clinics termed "shopping clinics," became popular as a forum for local physicians and clinics to bill the government for a variety of services from inner city patrons, services they most likely did not need. The New York Medicaid system in particular functioned with a card that allowed a patient to be seen by a variety of doctors with little regard for their actual physical needs. Clinics became greedy with the government's "open checkbook," and it wasn't long before my mother, operating as the clinic's "ghost" administrator, learned to drain the system with the best of them. Her newfound knowledge opened the door for a wealth of opportunities, and it wasn't long before those opportunities began to be revealed.

Following my mother's divorce, I had been allowed to stay in Miami with family friends in order to finish high school, but the agreement was that immediately following graduation I would return to New York and live in Queens with her. The family that housed me in Miami had a daughter my age and she and I quickly became the best of friends. Upon graduating from high school she and I both headed up to Queens and began to work at the clinic in Harlem beside my mother. The idea was for us to get valuable medical field training and earn enough money to eventually pay for college. According to this plan, I would work as a medical assistant. My mother's hopes were that I would get the necessary exposure to launch my dream of entering into a career in the medical field.

Although from a professional perspective everything appeared to be falling into place, my new home life in the city was not. The temptations of the New York City lifestyle with its Latin night clubs and popular drug scene were permeating my journey into adulthood. My mother's casual affair with the "real" clinic administrator was also causing unintended disruptions to my already somewhat chaotic lifestyle. It was odd as we actually became close family friends not only to my mother's lover but to his wife and child. His wife refused to see the reality of events unfolding around her and I bore a great deal of guilt and condemnation as I came to care about her and was not at all in agreement with my own mother's actions with this woman's husband.

Over the next six months after my initial arrival, life in New York quickly began to fall apart. My childhood best friend became homesick and not even the excitement of the Manhattan lifestyle could make her stay. After only three months she returned home to Miami and I was left alone. My desire to attend school began to wane and I was instead becoming more and more heavily involved in using uppers and alcohol as part of the nightly party scene.

Genuinely concerned about the direction I was heading in; my mother grudgingly relented and allowed me to move back to Miami. Her lover's wife had taken a secondary motherly role in my life and an opportunity arose for her to start a new business in the fabric industry with family members in Miami. She invited me to come along in the mean time, while she waited for her husband to join her. In essence, she and I would be leaving the city and providing my own mother and her lover all the room to continue with their torrid affair. I had my suspicions that this woman was not as naïve as she presented herself to be and was well aware of the situation going on in her own home. Moving to Miami seemed to be a way for her to step away from the tragic situation she was in and provide her with both an escape and opportunities. She must have felt sorry for me and realized that I, too, needed desperately to escape. She was right and without a moment's hesitation I packed my bags and followed her back to the sunny beaches of beautiful Miami, Florida.

It was time to place all of the dysfunction and chaos of New York City behind me and start fresh in paradise. Determined and excited to experience my newfound freedom away from the watchful eyes of my domineering mother, I enrolled in Miami Dade College and answered a newspaper ad seeking a receptionist at a *Women's Clinic* close by the house where I was staying. I was immediately hired and began my training on how to answer the phone behind the front desk. At the time, all I was looking for was a job and an opportunity. Being offered a position in a medical clinic was a great opportunity as it allowed me to stay in the medical field, where I hoped to continue to grow and develop.

I was not familiar with the services offered by this clinic at the time I accepted the job. I assumed with it being a women's clinic, it implied annual gynecological exams and birth control. It wasn't until I was hired that I discovered they also provided abortions. I was unfamiliar with the medical procedure itself as it related to abortions, but three years before *Roe V. Wade* had made abortions legal and to my impressionable young mind legal meant that they were safe. As far as I was concerned that was really all that mattered.

Only two months into my employment I was involved in a serious car accident and forced to take a leave of absence from work. At the same time my mother and her lover, my current caretaker's husband, arrived to live in Miami. With the vacancy I was leaving at the clinic, I suggested my mother apply for my job at the Women's Clinic. She did and was immediately hired to replace me. However, answering phones and managing front desk operations was not going to satisfy the headstrong, entrepreneurial woman I knew and admired. It was only a couple of weeks before she took the initiative to delve back into the operations of the clinic and learn how the money was being made.

Her motives unknown to them, the doctors welcomed my mother's interest and initiative. They shared with her viable information in the daily billing and cash collection of their clinic. They had no idea the extent of the formidable force within their midst. It wasn't long before she began planning the opening of her own center, where she would soon become their biggest competitor.

Shortly after learning the ins and outs of the abortion business, and discovering what a lucrative business it was, she purchased a condominium in a new development of the growing suburb called Hialeah. She then set out to find the busiest intersection in the quickly growing city and purchased an office space that would be renovated into an abortion center.

This was an exciting time for my mother. She was finally going to realize her dream of running her own operation. She obtained financing for her project by selling a plot of land in Puerto Rico, left to her by her parents. With that money she immediately began putting up dry wall and renovating the area's newest abortion center.

She had witnessed firsthand the demand for termination with the newly implemented federal approval of the laws. It was an opportunity she was ready to cash in on. With a fierce determination and a relentless pursuit to launch her new business, it wasn't long before Hialeah's newest abortion center opened on 390 West 49th Street and immediately began to serve the hundreds of confused and distraught women in Miami looking to choose death for their unborn babies.

CHAPTER THREE

All Roads Lead to Hialeah
Hialeah, Florida

The History

The city of Hialeah, FL, nestled diagonally northwest from the heart of the city of Miami, rests as part of Miami-Dade County. A city named after the Seminole word for *high prairie*, its foundation for inhabitance began in 1916 with the implementation of a landing strip for the area's first flying school and residential community.

The early "Roaring 20's" made their mark in the area. The small prairie town alongside the Everglades hosted the region's premier golf course, greyhound race track, and motion picture studio called the *Miami Studios Motion Picture Complex*. The small town's economy, with a population of only fifteen hundred, had big prospects. The area's growth and development was on the forefront of its resident's minds until the great hurricane in September of 1926 devastated nearly seventy percent of the homes and caused upwards of $31 million dollars in property damage. With the subsequent onslaught of the Great Depression, the land boom in Florida came to a halt and prospects for the surrounding areas became bleak.

True to form, the spirit of the people in the area rebounded, resolute in redeveloping their beloved city and a plan to rebuild began. In 1932, Philadelphia horse racing enthusiast Joseph E. Widener took a chance on the area, investing in the local economy by completely rebuilding the Miami Jockey Club, a two hundred twenty acre park and race horse track that received more coverage in the Miami media than any other sporting event in the history of Miami up to that time. In 1937 the park hosted the famous Amelia Earhart as she bid farewell to the United States and embarked upon her final tragic flight around the globe.

The 1940's brought about a new era for Hialeah as the manufacturing industry began widespread development in the area. By 1945 twenty-six manufacturing businesses were operating within the small city to include the transformation of the old Miami Studios into a factory for portable, pre-fabricated frame houses. With the production of affordable homes, the removal of the personal property tax in the area, and the growth of light industry, Hialeah began to standout out as an ideal relocation spot for the immigrating Cubans in the 1950's. As the city's leaders began to taste the profits of growth and commercialization, Hialeah repealed the inventory tax in 1955, drawing even more viability as a manufacturing and distribution center.

By the time the city entered the 1960's, Hialeah had become well known as a city of opportunity for the quickly growing Latin population. This decade represented abundance and growth for the small now predominantly Latin community. Fidel Castro's 1959 revolution opened the flood gates to thousands of fleeing Cubans searching for an opportunity in the United States. Local manufacturing businesses were providing those with the dream to thrive in America the opportunity to relocate to the area and surround themselves with people of similar origin. In this city they could find a steady paying job that matched the locally low priced cost of living.

By 1970 the US Census reported Hialeah's population at over one hundred thousand for the very first time. By 1975, fifty-two percent of that population was of Latin descent, primarily Cuban. Today it's considered the second highest percentage of Cuban and Cuban American residents of any city in the country.

Peter Pan Project (Operation Pedro Pan)

Serving as one of the great influxes of Cuban children in the nearby region was an initiative called Operation Pedro Pan which took effect from December of 1960 – October of 1962. Recorded as the "largest exodus of unaccompanied minors in the Western Hemisphere," this was a strategy for the Cuban parents fearing indoctrination and loss of their parental authority, to choose how their children would be educated.

In the course of almost two years, nearly fourteen thousand unaccompanied minors were sent from Cuba to the shores of Miami searching for freedom and a chance to achieve the American dream. Nearly fifty percent of them had no friends or family to receive them, but because of the efforts of the CWB of Miami and Operation Pedro Pan these young people were well cared for. Eighty-five percent of the boys in the custody of the CWB were between the ages of twelve to eighteen. They reached adulthood shortly after arriving in Miami and then became independent. Some never reunited with their families.

In 1962 the commercial flights between Cuba and the United States ceased with the Cuban Missile Crisis and for the next three years travel was conducted through Spain and Mexico. In 1965 the initiation of Freedom Flights began as a compromise between the US and Cuban government, solely for the purpose of reuniting families. Parents of unaccompanied minors were given first priority. This helped to reunite the majority still in the care of the CWB with their families.

It is necessary to note the great sacrifice made by the parents of these children as they risked giving them up completely, if necessary, in order to preserve their children's right to the best possible life. In this case it was a life liberated from the threat of the Marxist-Leninist indoctrination, a threat only strengthened by the Cuban government's closing of Catholic and private schools in 1961. Further, there was a push toward the "literacy campaign" which would force children over the age of thirteen to enter into Cuba's rural areas and focus on teaching basic reading and writing to the area's illiterate population using materials that would continue to propagate the ideals of *The Revolution*.

It is with this example that I hope to share the stark difference in mindset of the vulnerable Cuban people. On the one side, they were committing the greatest of sacrifices to offer life to their children, even if it meant giving them up to the foreign United States. On the other hand they were using that same ideology of sacrifice as a justification to choose death for the unborn.

The Clinic

In 1977, my mother and I located an available building on one of Hialeah's busiest intersections. The population in the area, especially the Cuban population, was continuing to grow. What was unique about this particular group was the desperation that embodied who they were. This city was plagued with an urgency to progress at any cost. After successfully overcoming so much in seeking stability of life in America, many were raised to believe that a pregnancy, under any circumstances, and the responsibilities associated with a pregnancy, would only destroy the progress they'd made thus far.

From a business standpoint this was an ideal target market for the new clinic. My mother and her business partner understood the majority mindset of the Latin community as it related to progress. The ambivalent woman and her loved ones were susceptible to the idea that a pregnancy would impede their personal progress. The goal of the clinic was simply to guide the discussion with the patients towards the benefits of future opportunities without the burden of an unplanned or unwanted baby. This discussion would occur once the pregnancy tests were done - but not necessarily with a confirmed pregnancy.

With a business strategy firmly in place, the stage was set for our new location to make its mark on the community. In September of 1977 the corner sign was raised ten feet up toward the oncoming traffic and lit brightly for all to see. It welcomed the masses to the *Hialeah Medical Center for Women.* It deceptively presented "opportunity and care" for the many potential mothers and fathers who walked through its doors unsure about their options. But the staff ensured that they would be convinced that terminating the pregnancy would be the sole option for a real chance at the American dream.

CHAPTER FOUR

A Business Venture
THE CLINIC

The grand opening of her clinic fueled my mother's every thought, discussion and action. As far as she was concerned, money was no object. Her bank account, on the other hand, reflected differently, especially after selling her inheritance, a one and a half acre parcel in Puerto Rico, for ten thousand dollars. But she was not about to allow something as trivial as limited funds and an unfunded budget affect her dream to build a world class clinic. This project was destined to reflect her ruthless ambitions. Her dismissal of costs and expenses raised the stakes and stress in an already tumultuous relationship with her business partner/married lover. Their fighting was endless. There were times when it seemed the discord between the two of them might impact the success of the business they ventured toward together.

Looking back now, I can see where the establishment of this clinic was a move in a game of chess the enemy made toward waging war on Miami's front lines. He was working overtime to ensure its emplacement. Initially, he was successful.

In June of 1978 the doors to the *Hialeah Medical Center for Women* officially opened. It was one of the first abortion clinics in the growing city. With one operating room and two Cuban doctors, the stage was set to begin terminating unwanted pregnancies for the women who felt lost, confused or placed in what they believed to be impossible circumstances. Immediately following the grand opening the clinic began to see an average of four to five women per day for procedures costing between one hundred seventy-five to three hundred dollars, determined by how far along they were in their pregnancy – the further along, the higher the cost.

Often times the women would enter the clinic just to get a pregnancy test. If the test was positive, the staff was trained to council her to either begin the paperwork or return the very same day in order to terminate the pregnancy. The more time that passed from the confirmation of the pregnancy, the higher the chance the clinic would lose the revenue associated with the patient. The key to profit was to conduct as many procedures as possible, which required guiding these women toward abortion immediately.

Ultrasound was not yet commonly used. So the staff resorted to the use of a measuring tape to determine the gestational age of the fetus. This antiquated and unreliable method gave us a somewhat educated guess as to the approximate number of weeks along the patient was in her pregnancy. If the patient was less than eight weeks, calculated by the date of her last menstrual cycle and tape measure, a vaginal exam was conducted to determine the size of the uterus. This also helped to provide a "best guess" as to the gestational age of the fetus. Unfortunately, without an ultrasound machine, neither of these two practices determined if there were multiple fetuses in the womb. It wouldn't be until after the actual abortion was conducted that the mother would be made aware of, if applicable, her now deceased multiple fetuses.

It was also common to counsel women to abort their pregnancies when the pregnancy tests proved inconclusive. This was not considered unethical or illegal in any fashion by our medical team. In fact, I can recall one of our physicians stating that the patient "wouldn't know the difference," after having undergone a procedural abortion, although there was no evidence to prove she was, in fact, pregnant. As far as the doctor was concerned, his technique, at a minimum, regulated her menstrual cycle and provided necessary dollars for the success of the clinic.

It was a money-making business and no one ever considered "taking their eyes off the prize" and seeing instead the broken hearts of the women that lay there on the operating table, losing or believing to have lost a piece of their own soul.

The Procedure

When it came to the actual procedure, the medical technology was not as advanced as it is today. The actual terminations were very invasive and required constant medical oversight. The option of administering Mifepristone, also known as the RU-486 hormone blocker, and expelling your baby in the comfort of your own home or bathroom was not on the market; therefore patients underwent medical procedures within the walls of a clinic.

Our general practice was to have the nurse begin the procedure by intravenously administering a barbiturate known as sodium thiopental, better known as Sodium Pentothal or "truth serum." This medication is well known for its use as the first of three injections in the majority of death sentences administered via injection. As a barbiturate it is used to depress the central nervous system to produce hypnosis and anesthesia without analgesia (the inability to feel pain). The patient is normally rendered unconscious within thirty seconds of administration as it is absorbed immediately by the brain.

It was common for an anesthesiologist to put a patient to sleep for any abortion procedure, including the vacuum aspiration method. Today things are different. It is less risky for the medical staff to use a local anesthetic rather than place a patient under general anesthesia. Therefore, for the vacuum aspiration methods currently in use, patients are generally wide awake and can feel pain throughout the procedure. They are also aware of the happenings in the operating room, including the noise of the machine. This has been known to cause phobia and manic episodes in some patients when they later hear a sound like a standard household vacuum cleaner.

However, during our procedures patients were placed under general anesthesia as the doctor dilated the cervix. Using the aspiration machine and forceps he would remove all contents of her womb. The procedure itself (no commas) normally took only a few minutes. No one placed any thought on the years of emotional distress it would cause the patient. As far as everyone was concerned, we were helping her and her potential for the future.

Once the procedure was complete the patient was allowed to rest and recover in a separate recovery room located near the back of the building. Six cots were placed stationary against the wall. There were varying reactions from the women as they lay there processing their newfound reality. Some were quiet, others cried, others looked utterly confused and unsure because everything going on around them seemed to be happening so fast.

We had a back door that led to the outside directly from that room. It allowed the women to exit the building without having to return through the front door. The last thing we wanted were grief stricken women with tearstained cheeks to exit through the front door and be seen by potential clientele. We could not risk anyone witnessing these women as they left the building gripping their bellies in pain as they howled with loss. These reactions had to be kept private or it could pose a threat to our expanding market.

At the end of the day we all agreed that what we were doing day to day was in perfect accordance with the law, which clearly meant that we were not doing anything wrong. It was a basic business operation. There was a demand for a service and my mother and I worked together to provide that service for a fee. We weren't luring people to the clinic under false pretenses. We were giving them exactly what they wanted and the money we were making as a result only helped to justify our rationalizations. What could possibly be wrong with finding a niche market and realizing the American dream of owning a successful company?

It seemed so simple. Our rationalizations were very black and white. There was no clear breaking of the law therefore, there was no harm. We couldn't begin to understand the impact of the seeds we were sowing in our community. The harvest that was approaching was one none of us wanted to see coming. It was only a matter of time...

CHAPTER FIVE
There Was No Denying
THE WOMEN

Business was booming from a quantity standpoint. Each month that passed allowed more and more women to walk through our doors. Some were certain about their choice, at least in the short term, while others were still unsure, but vulnerable to our persistent efforts to control their decisions. Deep in my heart something felt very wrong about what we were doing, but I allowed my desires to succeed quell those troublesome feelings. I had prestige; I was the daughter of the clinic's owner, a position of power among doctors and medical staff. Yet it was all of superficial value. From a financial perspective the clinic was struggling. Regardless of the increases in patient volume our finances were never in the green. It seemed as though no matter how much money was coming in, it was never enough.

Without the security of sufficient revenue, we – my mother and I - were required to spend countless hours, the majority of our waking hours at the clinic.

It was there that I saw them and heard their stories. It was there that I witnessed the pain they had in their sunken eyes. At the time I chose to turn away from them in ignorance. It felt easier to be a part of this business if I didn't ask too many questions. I didn't want to know why any of the women were in our clinic. Their circumstances were of no interest to me. I had to find a way to become numb to it all, so I feigned disinterest.

And yet there was no denying the reality. Day after day, so many women walked through our doors and stood in line like cattle being led to slaughter. In truth, that analogy seems tragically appropriate. We believed we were running a successful business, providing a location with services that were in demand by the local community, but in truth we were running a slaughter house, a place of execution for the unborn.

I can't honestly share the story of the center and our role in this travesty without sharing a few examples of the women we saw, the few I was unable to ignore. I hope to accurately reflect the truth behind the daily happenings in an abortion center. It isn't pretty and it isn't simple. It's life and it's death. And it's time we speak up and begin sharing the truth.

The Rape Victim

When she first walked in, we were all appalled by one mother's choice. She was an African American woman that boldly entered into the waiting room with a small child clutching her mother's rather large fist. The little girl couldn't have been more than nine years old and she appeared terrified as she clung to her mother with one hand and to a stuffed teddy bear with the other.

Surely, there had to be someone that could provide childcare locally, we reasoned, in order to spare the little girl the experience of witnessing her mother terminate a pregnancy. We found it was completely inappropriate and unacceptable that a child be allowed in the waiting room, not to mention the potential discomfort it could have caused our other patients still waiting to complete their own procedures.

As the solemn woman approached the front desk to sign in we explained that we could not allow for a child to accompany a patient. She would not be in any condition to care for that child immediately following the abortion due to the sedatives that would still be in her system. The mother sadly whispered that her child *was* the patient.

Those of us behind the front desk swallowed our alarm and attempted to maintain our professionalism as we silently handed her a stack of forms to fill out. The little girl's big brown eyes looked around in confusion and disbelief. She rested her tiny little head on her mother's arm and brought the stuffed teddy bear closer to her heart as she silently waited for the finished forms to be processed and for her turn to come up.

She was only nine years old. An innocent and blameless child who'd been raped by a family member. She and her mother had driven all the way to Miami from Georgia in order to terminate the pregnancy. And as I witnessed the rounded belly beneath her clothes, my heart broke at the evil that was in this world.

She trembled throughout the initial examination. Tears silently slipped down her cheeks, as she looked at all of us, confused by what was happening to her. We discovered that she was four months along and would have to undergo a dilation and evacuation procedure also known as a D&E abortion. This would require placing her under general anesthesia and doing the procedure in a two-step process requiring an overnight treatment.

No one at the center involved in her case could escape the emotional impact this particular patient had on us all. On the one hand it appeared as though we were doing her a just service. She'd been raped. She never intended to get pregnant. She was only a baby. The results of this rape were only going to perpetuate an already tragic situation and force her to relive the experience, at minimum, for another five months until the baby was born. We had the chance to spare her from all that and end her pain that day. It seemed to be a crystal clear decision and we immediately began making preparations for her procedure.

That I evening I sat with her.

She was such a tiny young girl weighing no more than seventy-five pounds. I studied her small frame dressed in an oversized operating gown. She was hooked up to an IV; her swollen belly rose and fell with each labored breath. Her tiny feet were swallowed by the metal of the table's stirrups. I remember the lump that formed in my throat as I began to wonder if this was truly the best option for her. Obviously, I kept all of my personal opinions and internal conflicts to myself, but it didn't stop me from wondering if by aborting her unborn child we weren't adding more trauma and loss to an already devastating situation. I imagined this little girl waking up to feel something missing inside of her. We would then have to explain that her baby was no longer there. How do you explain to a nine year old that none of this is her fault? How can she understand that, although the legal option to have an abortion implies that women are given a choice, she never really had a choice at all? Instead, the adults in her life were making that choice for her.

It was the first time that I began to realize that legality didn't necessarily imply ethical soundness.

Near Death

No story of a clinic, hospital, or surgical center would be complete without its stories of near death experiences. However, I highlight this one story in particular because we are so often told that abortions are nearly "no risk procedures" and are preferable to childbirth in terms of risk factors. I have witnessed something very different.

There was a young woman in her early twenties. She didn't have any children and had opted to terminate her first pregnancy.

As far as her case was concerned everything fell within the standard and normal range. She was less than twelve weeks pregnant and in good health. . There was no way to foresee what would happen next.

The anesthesiologist administered the sodium pentothal, which was part of our standard procedure, when she appeared to develop an allergic reaction and went into respiratory arrest.

It was only a matter of seconds before I witnessed the doctor jump up and literally begin pounding on her chest trying to revive her before she died on the operating table. She was asphyxiating and it quickly began to seem hopeless. She was going to die.

Thankfully we experienced God's grace that day, and she did not die but finally began to breathe on her own. She recovered quickly enough for the doctor to continue her abortion. That afternoon she was informed of what had happened and told she was lucky to be alive. Her baby, however, was not.

The Chronic Patient

Initially, my heart broke for a young, beautiful Cuban woman with long black hair that hung nearly to her waist. She gracefully made her way through the waiting room to the receptionist at the front desk. She shared with us her tragic story of having escaped the oppression of the Caribbean island in search of a dream to become a successful woman in the United States. She was working diligently to learn English and was preparing to enroll in college when she discovered that she was pregnant.

She was not married and there was no serious relationship in her life. Her pregnancy was the result of a casual fling with a man at a nightclub. She was adamant that mothering a child was not in line with her plans or dreams for her life. Although there was no reason for her to share all of this information, she appeared as though she needed someone to talk to. It was good business for us to maintain high levels of customer service, so we listened.

Sadly, her first termination appeared to be a gateway procedure for many future visits. With four other sisters and only a father to raise them, she appeared to have more deeply rooted issues than anyone at our clinic was trained to understand.

We willingly treated her for three additional procedures before the physicians at the clinic finally made it clear that they were unwilling to treat her again. If she was going to continue to get pregnant and terminate her pregnancies she would have to find somewhere else to have her procedures done.

The woman who left the center after her fourth procedure was not the same woman who'd arrived right before the first. Something had changed inside her. She wasn't as talkative anymore, instead appearing sullen and angry. When the staff greeted her she barely looked any of them in the eye. It was obvious she wanted to get things done and over with. I can only describe her transition as sorrowful as we watched someone so full of life and personality, become an empty shell.

The Woman under Pressure

One woman in particular's story was devastating as she worked up the courage to do what she felt those around her thought she should do. It was obvious by the look in her eyes and the tightness of her lips that she was not sure at all about having an abortion.

When she arrived at the clinic there were no other patients, but the waiting room was filled with an entourage of people that would be impacted if she didn't go through with the procedure, including the unborn child's father who was adamantly opposed to her keeping the baby.

She repeatedly took deep breaths and stared at the various corners in the room, visibly willing herself to another place in her mind. She didn't say more than a word or two. She simply signed the forms and continued taking deep breaths. Those deep breaths were her way of fighting against the tears that threatened to spill over in agony over the death of her unborn baby.

The anesthesia had very little effect on her as even under the heavy barbiturate her body fought the procedure. The doctors became alarmed as her lower back writhed back and forth in resistance, rising up from the table as they attempted to empty the contents of her womb. The staff present during the process physically held her in order to complete the abortion and gave her an extra sedative to help calm her. Almost as soon as it had begun, it was over. This woman's choice had, too, been made for her and there was no undoing what was done.

As soon as she awoke from the procedure she cried in mourning for her lost child. There was anger mixed with hopelessness in her eyes as she stumbled, limping through the recovery room and out to the waiting vehicle where her boyfriend appeared relaxed and at ease. As far as he was concerned, his problems were over, only for her the real pain and grief had only just begun.

***

The woman under pressure was my own personal story.

I never expected that I, too, would become one of my mother's many patients, but that day it proved to be so. I loved my unborn baby. I didn't want to end my pregnancy, but the pressure to terminate was too overwhelming. With the convenience of a clinic at my disposal I succumbed to the pressure and chose my relationship with my boyfriend over the life of my child, a decision I instantly began to regret.

This clinic didn't just play a major role within the lives of the Hialeah community but within my own life as well. I experienced firsthand what the pain of the abortion was like for the hundreds of women that had walked through our doors. And while everyone reacts to trauma differently, my own experience began to open my eyes to the reality of what was going on around me within the walls of the business my mother and I had helped to create.

It was the beginning of the end, as I reflected on the reality of the magnitude of death that surrounded us - the endless killings that were taking place day after day right beside me. With the trauma of own my abortion fresh in my mind, my personal feelings began to change and I began to suffocate within the reality of what we had done and were continuing to do to the mostly Hispanic people of our own community.

This was the launching pad of what would continue to be more devastating effects in my life. The tragedies moved like falling dominos culminating in my own near death experience. Only then did I finally reach my hands up to the Heavens and ask for grace and forgiveness.

I am blessed today to say that not only did the Lord offer me his mercy, but in an even more beautiful gesture, he graced upon me a chance at redemption. But at the beginning of this journey my future didn't look very bright; it was actually a pathway through darkness and pain.

CHAPTER SIX

A Personal Connection

Jeanne's Story

My pregnancy was supposed to be the product of a love story. I had fallen deeply in love with a man who represented a type of father figure in my life. He was nearly twenty years my senior, but it was no surprise that after my tumultuous and dysfunctional relationship with my parents, I would be drawn to such a man.

He was a good looking and confident, Cuban born entrepreneur, whose savvy business sense and charismatic personality led him on a hard won journey to success. From humble beginnings as an educated immigrant who mopped floors at a local furniture store in Miami, to becoming the owner of that store, his ruthlessness and stubborn need to rise to the top proved instrumental in motivating him to achieve his goal of becoming a successful businessman. It wasn't long before he began expanding his own business holdings and sought out additional opportunities, becoming the owner of an import/export company. This, too, proved to be financially successful.

It was in his pursuit to seek even more investment opportunities that our paths crossed and he agreed to buy out my mother's forbidden lover and business partner at the clinic and become her new silent partner. This was an extremely beneficial situation for all parties as both my mother and her current partner knew that their relationship had reached its end, and her new partner agreed to allow her to run the clinic on her own. His only interest was making money. After familiarizing himself with the demographics of the area and a brief explanation of the business model, he felt confident that investing in the *Hialeah Medical Center for Women* would be a wise financial move.

I was excited about the prospects of this new partnership as I'd already become well acquainted with this man. When we first met through a mutual acquaintance, I was hired to accompany him on a trip to Venezuela as part of his import/export interests. I was to serve as a secretarial administrator. This allowed us to share intimate dinners together where we discussed the possibility of him investing in my mother's clinic.

I was very taken by the entire situation, being swept away to a South American country by a wealthy businessman who definitely knew how to entertain ladies. It was obvious that he had his sights on me and I was both flattered and foolishly disillusioned by the possibility of being the center of such a man's affections.

Shortly after the documents were signed and he was made my mother's business partner we moved into a whirlwind romance. I knew that he had a huge reputation as a lady's man, but I was young and naïve and made confident by his dedicated interest and displays of affection. There were definite warning signs. It was obvious that he was dedicated to his own success and self interests first and foremost, but I consciously chose to ignore my instincts and insist to myself that we could have a future. It wasn't long before I discovered that I was pregnant with his child. I was sure this would be the necessary binding between us and a decision would be made for us to marry and begin a family. I was very much in love and craved the opportunity to provide myself with a tight-knit family and a chance at a solid lifestyle for my own child - a foundation I'd never been given myself. Only my dreams quickly vanished.

As I mentioned in the earlier chapter, my boyfriend was less than thrilled with the news of my pregnancy. In fact, he was adamantly opposed to me carrying the baby to term. The news of my pregnancy highlighted the ruthless and callous nature of this man, qualities that had served him well on his rise in business, but made it impossible for him to warm to the idea of anything he felt might stop or slow his personal ambitions. Truth be told, I don't think he felt ready or compelled to settle down with one woman either. His desire to live that "playboy" lifestyle still played a dominant role in his character. A new baby just didn't fit into his picture of what his life should look like. As a result he was forcefully persistent that I terminate my pregnancy. As the new owner of our very own abortion clinic, the conditions were set for the procedure to be easy to obtain and as far as he was concerned it was a surefire solution to an unnecessary problem.

I allowed his pressure and disinterest to get the best of me, although deep in my heart of hearts, abortion was the last thing I wanted. But I was suffering both physically and emotionally from his rejection. I didn't feel as though I had any other option. I believed my pain, both internal and external, had probably already done substantial damage to my unborn baby. And so with a heavy heart and strong feelings that I should not terminate my pregnancy I allowed them to herd me into the operating room I knew so well. Thus, I became another one of the countless number of broken hearts that entered into the pen for slaughter.

My abortion was one of the greatest tragedies of my life. I cried endlessly and mourned the loss of the baby I'd already grown to love, a baby conceived with a man I also loved. It felt as though I was mourning both the life of my unborn child and the loss of a possibly beautiful future with this man. However, I still refused to fully give up and walk away from the relationship. After sacrificing so much in order to be with him, I felt that he owed me something. I wasn't yet willing to let him just walk away. Confident that our little problem was taken care of, he resumed our courtship as though nothing had ever happened. It was only a few short weeks later that I once again became pregnant.

Upon discovery of my pregnancy I was both thrilled and terrified. I was suffering something very common among post abortive women and that is the need to replace the child I'd lost. I had a physiological need to be pregnant; my womb craved the life it had cradled only a few short weeks before. Shortly after my procedure, in an answer to my prayers, my request was granted and I was once again with child, only this time no one was going to take my baby away from me.

I kept my pregnancy a secret through the entire first trimester, ensuring that I'd be too far along once everyone discovered my condition to allow termination to be an option. I held hopes that somehow our personal relationship could strengthen to the point where my baby's father would realize that ending the first pregnancy had been a mistake. I hoped he would rejoice alongside me for the gift of another chance.

Sadly that did not happen. On the contrary, the man that I loved so dearly was aghast when he discovered that I was once again pregnant and had kept it a secret. He accused me of manipulating the situation and trying to trap him. He even allowed some of the other women in his life to convince him that the child was most likely someone else's. He convinced himself that it had to be true as an excuse to reject his own flesh and blood.

Our relationship did not make it beyond the discovery of my pregnancy. Unfortunately, as much as I begged and pleaded, he refused to commit to me and his child and instead opted to abandon us both. Although his decision pained me in the deepest of places where women store their passions and ardor for their first love, I was at peace that I'd chosen to keep my baby and no one could ever make me regret that.

My beautiful baby girl was born on August 18, 1979. My labor was near painless, which was quite a surprise considering the physical reaction I'd had with the abortion less than a year before I was blessed to be sedated during her delivery and able to enjoy her entry into the world.

Our clinic had been operating for over two years, but the strained relationship with my daughter's father, who still served as my mother's business partner, and his rejection of her first grandchild, caused my mother to look for alternative business solutions. There were still hopes that perhaps after my daughter was born he might change his mind and return to unite us a family, but those hopes were short lived. He did come to see her after she was born, but his ruthless nature and all-consuming pride reared its ugly head and he refused to acknowledge her as his own. I had no doubt that he was her father; he'd been the only man in my life at the time of her conception. I made the decision to give her his last name and list him as the father on her birth certificate. One day, I reasoned, if she ever chose to seek him out, he'd have to answer directly to her for his decisions. My mother, however, found his rejection appalling and began to scout out opportunities to cut ties with him and seek a new clinic for herself.

In December of 1979, only three months after my daughter's birth, a deal was struck and my mother sold her half of the clinic to a family friend. She had already spotted another high traffic corner and was seeking to open up a second abortion clinic in the city of Hialeah. We were on the cutting edge of a high dollar industry and now after two years in the business, my mother refused to do anything else but capitalize on the readily available market in a business she now knew well.

Under the new owners the *Hialeah Medical Clinic for Women* remained open for the next two years, continuing to offer abortions for the women who walked through its doors, before finally shutting its doors. There was a falling out among the new owners and everyone walked away after the sale of the building to, ironically enough, a local OB/GYN, a deliverer of unborn babies into a new and often complicated world.

For my mother things began to get out of hand and the end of our involvement in the abortion business would come shortly. A very public news story about an incident that occurred in our clinic impacted the local community and all of Miami for months.

CHAPTER SEVEN

Ending the Legacy

IRENE

Irene's story was quite newsworthy. After operating her second clinic for only one year, a woman entered into Irene's clinic requesting to terminate her pregnancy. With a lack of technology there was a miscalculation as the physicians began the procedure. They quickly discovered that she was much further along in her pregnancy than originally thought. They had reached a point in the procedure where they would be forced to kill the very viable fetus at nearly thirty-two weeks gestation. The physicians worried the mother would change her mind given that she'd lied to the staff about how long she'd been pregnant. Further they questioned her mental stability. They considered the plausibility of ending the woman's life during what was already becoming a life threatening procedure, but Irene refused. Unwilling to commit murder within the walls of her clinic, she chose to fight to save the patient's life.

That evening every local news station covered the tragic circumstances of the woman nearly killed after an attempt was made to conduct a partial birth abortion at the local neighborhood abortion clinic. There were a slew of rumors that ran rampant for a short period of time including the questions about the role in this incident of the clinic's owner, who was not a physician. It generated substantial attention at the time, at least until the launch of the next big local news story.

Sadly Irene's situation would not be so temporary. An investigation was conducted and her clinic was shut down. Both Irene and her Argentinean husband were placed under arrest and sentenced to serve time at the local county jail.

With a dedicated practice in the Cuban voodoo religion of *Santeria*, Irene sought spiritual council before appearing before the courts. They encouraged her to release a flock of live chickens onto the courthouse steps. They assured her that this would offer her spiritual protection. She and her husband did as they were instructed, carefully following the guidance of the witch doctors. Attorneys watched in awe as they let loose a group of chickens decorated with ribbons of varying colors to run rampant along the courthouse steps.

That afternoon she was sentenced to serve one year in the Dade County Jail for practicing medicine without a license. Her efforts to save the woman's life, by administering the antibiotic, had cost her freedom. Despite the attorney's persuasive arguments about the amount of nursing experience Irene had obtained after years of working with the clinics in New York and Florida, there was no persuading the judge and her sentence was to begin immediately.

Over the next eight months she quietly served her time in jail. She slept through the majority of her days, accepting that everything that was once valuable in her life was now gone. Her husband had also been sentenced to a year in jail, but it didn't matter; as far as she was concerned their marriage was over. The clinic, the second abortion clinic she'd opened in Miami, was now closed. She had no money, no personal belongings, and no one who was waiting for her on the outside. The only things that remained with her in the confines of her cell were the memories of the women they had served day after day, and the remains of the decimated unborn babies.

It was during this desolation that Irene first came across the message of Christianity and the idea that the Lord had once walked upon the earth as a man, named Jesus Christ.

It would take nearly eight years, but following on the footsteps of her daughter Jeanne's salvation, Irene too, would journey on the path to admitting her guilt for her sins and asking for the Lord's forgiveness and presence within her own heart.

Almost immediately after seeking salvation through a life with Jesus things began to change for the better in Irene's life.

It was apparent that the Lord had destined a divine purpose for her life to include an opportunity for redemption. In 1991, at the age of fifty-two, nearly nine years after having run a successful abortion business and being deeply involved in the dark religion of voodoo, Irene found herself moving to Colorado to study at the Colorado Christian University. But her journey would not end there. She would continue to study and work in the ministry completing both a Masters degree in Divinity and a Doctorate degree in Christian Ministry from Oral Roberts University in Tulsa, Oklahoma.

Prior to beginning her PhD in 1999, Irene returned to the world of medicine, the world she'd once aspired to be a part of. Only this time she returned as a Chaplain, a healer through prayer. As she walked the halls of the hospital and visited the patients, she would share the good news of Christ and pray with them and their loved ones. Some of the patients were already followers of Christ, but others were led there by her gentle words of redemption and forgiveness.

It was through her perseverance and the grace and mercy of a loving Heavenly Father that the bonds of condemnation began to crumble and the building blocks for full redemption began in her life and in the generations after her. The time had not yet come, but it wouldn't be long before she would witness firsthand the glory of God, working through her very own daughter, Jeanne. She proudly watched as he chose what was once her very own building as a trophy for the pro-life forces in the Miami, FL abortion wars.

CHAPTER EIGHT

Moving on to a New Life
Jeanne's Story Part II

February 1980

The first six months of my daughter's life were consumed by my need to survive. I was distraught, heartbroken, and alone. I'd been abandoned by the first man I'd ever wanted to spend the rest of my life with. Yes, I was given a daughter from that experience, but I was still angry that she would be forced to grow up without a father.

Emotionally I was a vulnerable and pained mess. Every day became a strategy of coping and survival. I was working two jobs, trying to make ends meet, and pay for the small studio apartment my new baby and I were living in. I met a young and handsome man who managed the boutique where I'd recently begun working. He, too, was a Cuban immigrant, a former Merchant Marine in his home country who had just recently arrived in Miami. I was touched by his affection toward my seven month old baby girl. The first time he saw her he glanced at her in adoration and remarked what a beautiful baby she was. It was enough to capture my attention. His affections toward me and my daughter were, in essence, medicine for my broken heart. I didn't want my daughter to miss out on the experience of having a father who loved her. It was because of his affections toward her that I found myself quickly falling in love and entering into a new relationship. However, quite contrary to my previous relationship, the commitment between us moved very quickly and it was only a couple of months after we met that he was proposing that we move in together.

As I watched him bond with my daughter, my hopes that her biological father would return to our life receded and I was forced to accept my new reality. I'd met what appeared to be a good man, and he was offering me what I'd claimed to so desperately want – a family.

Our beginnings weren't without challenges. The whole community faced problems with the release of the prisoners and mental patients from Cuba via "The Mariel Release." But that in turn brought not only his older brother, but also a woman from a previous relationship he'd had in Cuba. It was a time when I wasn't sure if our relationship would survive, but somehow it did and he chose me.

The arrival of his family in need, the decision to move forward with our relationship, and the fact that I had a small child to support all began to put pressure on us both and it wasn't long before he began to get mixed up with people that were deeply involved in drug smuggling. With the burden of being unable to speak English and the lack of any formal US education or transferable degree, my fiancé felt the temptations of opportunities to make large sums of money with little effort. It wasn't long before he'd committed to taking some very serious risks and moving large amounts of drugs from Miami to New York City.

The drug cartel wasn't the only thing that entered into my life as a result of my relationship. I also began to visit a spiritualist or a Cuban version of a fortune teller, known for his involvement in *Santeria,* the same form of voodoo once practiced by my mother. As sin would have it, this particular spiritualist had found a lucrative opportunity serving as a point of communication among the drug smugglers. Masked as a fortune teller and spiritual counselor, he was making large strides in the world of connecting likeminded individuals who were interested in passing drugs up and down the Eastern coast of the United States. Through him, my fiancé began to make key contacts and the money began rolling in.

Shortly after his new lucrative career began to take off, I discovered that I was once again pregnant. Only this time I'd managed to get pregnant with an intrauterine device (IUD) firmly in place. The doctor had assured me that there was a less than one percent chance I'd conceive with this particular form of birth control. Somehow, I'd managed to defy the odds and ended up pregnant anyway. With this discovery, the doctor informed us that because of the IUD there was a risk the baby could turn out to be a special needs child. I could see the concern on his face as he broached the subject of possibly terminating the pregnancy. The mere thought brought terror to my heart as I relived my previous experience and I made myself abundantly clear that termination was not an option.

Realizing that this was not a debatable decision, we braced ourselves for the birth of our child and in July of

1982 we welcomed a healthy and beautiful baby girl. It was a high point in our lives where money was no object.

The nursery for our new daughter was decorated in gold and lace. We were living in a brand new townhouse in one of the nicer sections of Miami and I was driving a new Cadillac. Overall, life was crowned with the sparkles of my gold jewelry, but it didn't take long until our house of cards came tumbling down.

Only three months after the birth of our daughter, I was robbed at gunpoint by rivals of my husband's cartel. He was in Houston, Texas, negotiating the terms of a "once in a lifetime" deal that would set us up for years. The robbery cleaned us out of all the money and jewelry we owned. To add to the turmoil the deal in Houston did not pan out, and instead arrests were made of the people initially involved. They named my husband as a participant and although he'd managed to escape back to Miami, we knew there wasn't much time. It wouldn't be long before law enforcement would come looking for us. So we packed a few of our things. We were now penniless as a result of the robbery, and forced to travel with two small children, making the long drive to New York City. We held hopes for new opportunities among friends working for mirroring cartels.

I began to feel the familiar pangs of morning sickness as we drove up the east coast toward New York. My new baby girl was only six months old. Drudgingly I forced myself to head to the drug store during an overnight stop and purchase a pregnancy test.

It only took a few seconds before the test came back with an undeniable read of – pregnant. A third baby.

I was terrified. For someone who was so adamantly opposed to abortion, I allowed myself, for just a brief moment, to consider the possibility. Our life was in a state of chaos and instability. Nothing seemed more illogical than to have another baby. But immediately I began to relive the moments following my first abortion and something in my spirit told me that this baby would be my son. I could not risk taking the life of my one and only baby boy. No matter how hard it would be, I needed to find a way. So I made the decision to choose life and have my baby. I made my peace with the idea that as soon as he was born I would tie my tubes and end my ability to ever have children again. This allowed me the strength to do what at the time felt impossible and continue with my pregnancy.

We finally arrived in New York and spent three days in a downtown hotel waiting to meet with the buyers. On the morning they were scheduled to arrive I stepped out to buy breakfast and upon returning to the hotel with coffee and bagels in hand, discovered men in uniform swarming the lobby. By sheer grace and mercy I was able to get to our room and warn my husband, thus allowing us a few seconds to flush any incriminating evidence before fists pounded on our door demanding entry. We were able to escape that situation unscathed as there was no incriminating evidence in our room. The associates we were there with, in an adjacent room, were not so lucky; plenty of arrests were made. I was fully aware of how close we'd come to being hauled off to prison. The mere thought of delivering my baby in prison and losing custody of my two daughters was enough to scare me into submission. It was time to change our life and do things differently. We decided to stay with some friends in New York, tap into the welfare system, and try to find a better way.

We began our new journey with good intentions. God knows my heart simply wanted stability for my little family. Unsure of what to do next, we opted to rent a small apartment in the same building where a former high school friend of mine lived. She served as a life-line for me as I watched my belly grow, confined in a small apartment with my two young girls. My husband was repeatedly absent as he sought more and more opportunities to make a quick deal. Except it wasn't just about business for him anymore; the nightlife was seductive and he was spending more and more time at the city's nightclubs. He was seduced by debauchery that could only satisfy the demonic spirits I'd welcomed into my home. I had continued to seek guidance and support from the Cuban spiritualist and his array of voodoo spirits from the underworld.

Although my time running the abortion clinic had been plagued with tragedy and death, I'd managed to maintain an emotional detachment from the daily happenings going on around me. At least until I was the one lying on the operating table. Even then, however, my life was not quite as dark and tragic as it was living in a dark apartment in a poor section of the Bronx, once again abandoned by the man I loved. It was only, once again, by God's grace that I was able to survive that experience as I reached a point of near death. I'd gained very little weight during my pregnancy and yet still managed to deliver a healthy baby boy, but my own health after delivery continue to deteriorate as I battled with clinical depression. My husband had come close to abandoning us and moving on with another woman. The bleakness of my situation was more than I could bear. Wondering how I would survive alone with three small children I began to consider taking my own life. I was plagued with seductive thoughts of death and destruction by the very spirits I was welcoming into my home and my marriage. The seeds sewn in my life up to that point had been of greed, power, death, and idolatry and it threatened to destroy me completely.

But amidst the darkness shone the unwavering faithfulness of an all-merciful God. I met a guardian angel who introduced herself to me while the two of us were waiting in line at a bank. She began to talk to me about the power of believing in Jesus Christ. In what seemed like a whirl of activities, this woman and a group of other Christians entered our apartment and began to pray for me and my husband. It was a miracle in itself that he allowed them upstairs into our home, but the Holy Spirit was moving in our lives. My heart was so open to the peace and tranquility that these people offered.

Shortly after we prayed the prayer of salvation with the group, our immediate surroundings began to change and I followed up my newfound faith by being baptized. The inner peace that I experienced was so profoundly different from anything I'd ever come across in the past.

I began to realize that I'd somehow stumbled upon the true creator of the Heavens and the Earth. My obedience and willing heart began to reveal itself within our day-to-day lives. My husband also began to change; he put an end to his extramarital affair and began preparing us to finally leave New York City and return to Miami as a united family. It was awe- inspiring to see such a drastic turnaround in our lives resulting from the deepest desires of my heart, communicated through late night prayer sessions and fasting. God was hearing my prayers and, despite all I'd been involved with up to that point, he was faithful. He was facilitating the steps necessary to turn things around so that I could begin to fulfill his purpose for my life.

As we boarded the plane to Miami, I whispered a prayer of thanks to be finally leaving the strongholds of sin that ensnared us for so long in New York. I was ready and prepared for a new life with a newfound faith.

Sadly the deathly spirits of darkness were not to relent so easily and it wasn't long before our former spiritual advisor found his way back into my husband's life in Miami and proposed a final "once in a lifetime deal." It would require that my husband complete one final drug run from Miami to New York City.

I begged him not to go, but the temptations and the demonic pressures were too great, and he succumbed to Satan's enticements. Only a few short hours later I was notified that he'd been arrested in the state of Delaware and was being transferred to Texas where a warrant was out for his arrest from his previous trip to Houston.

I landed on my knees in prayer as the ground beneath my feet began to give way. This was my rock bottom, but I was not alone. The Lord was in control in my life. I'd already given up my heart and my life to him and once again he was faithful. During a full night of fasting and prayer I was given the following scripture as I sought guidance and wisdom from Heaven:

2 Chronicles 7:21-18
The LORD appeared to him at night and said:

"I have heard your prayer and have chosen this place for myself as a temple for sacrifices.

[13] "When I shut up the heavens so that there is no rain, or command locusts to devour the land or send a plague among my people, [14] if my people, who are called by my name, will humble themselves and pray and seek my face and turn from their wicked ways, then I will hear from heaven, and I will forgive their sin and will heal their land. [15] Now my eyes will be open and my ears attentive to the prayers offered in this place. [16] I have chosen and consecrated this temple so that my Name may be there forever. My eyes and my heart will always be there.

[17] "As for you, if you walk before me faithfully as David your father did, and do all I command, and observe my decrees and laws, [18] I will establish your royal throne, as I covenanted with David your father when I said, 'You shall never fail to have a successor to rule over Israel.'

[61]

I continued to pray and receive his word that I needed to repent, change my life. He would then restore the priesthood in my house. He directed me to a scripture directly above in 2 Chronicles 7:10 which listed a specific date – *23 of July* as the date of my victory.

I was not sure what all of this meant, but I was fully aware of God's promise in my life and I began to wait and be faithful, believing that something powerful was going to happen. I also focused on my own personal survival as I worked as a medical assistant with a local podiatrist and focused on the care and well being of my three children. It was a time of stillness as I waited for the Lord to guide my path.

He did not take long to answer.

After a short trip to El Paso, Texas, a small desert-like west Texas town nestled against the Franklin Mountains, things began to fall into place. It looked as though the prison where my husband would be housed would be in this small city. In a matter of moments it was clear that the Lord was leading me and my children to begin a new life there - far, far away from everything we'd ever known up to that point.

In a series of miracles, I finally arrived with my children and a friend who opted to be my travel companion and support system. When I first arrived, the authorities transferred my husband to Houston for sentencing, but when he finally returned to the facility in El Paso, I fell to my knees in tears and rejoicing. It was the first time since his arrest that my little family was all together again within the same city. The date he arrived was the 23rd of July, 1987, just as the Lord had promised me ten months before while directing me to 2 Chronicles 7:10. That's when I knew I was exactly where he called me to be and I would choose to walk the rest of my life following the Lord's guidance and calling.

This was only the beginning of a sixteen year journey through my own walk in the desert where I would be prepared physically, mentally, and emotionally for the greatest story of my life, the story of redemption in the little town of Hialeah, Florida for the atrocities I'd helped begin.

CHAPTER NINE

A Walk, Through the Desert
Jeanne's Story Part III

Sixteen years. I had no idea it would be that long, but my timing was not the Lord's timing and his timing is ultimately perfect.

To tell all of the stories of my tests and trials while living in El Paso, Texas would require another book entirely. I want to focus here on the highlights that helped build the road that led back to Jesus's divine plan for my life. This was the story that would eventually come full circle, back to what I'd once planted of sin and destruction and offer me a chance to harvest life instead. As Christ's many parables illustrate, I couldn't reap grace and life with the seeds I'd once planted. First, I needed to uproot the destruction within my own spirit and become a new creation, so that then and only then, would I be prepared to till the fertile soil of repentance and plant seeds of life.

This began with my own spiritual healing. My husband spent the next three years after my arrival in El Paso incarcerated. It was truly a miracle that he was let out so soon. I spent the majority of those three years wondering if I would ever see him as a free man again. But rather than allow my earthly eyes dictate my circumstances, I walked in faith believing that God would perform a miracle honoring my faith and obedience.

I began a newfound relationship with a very special church in the area, a church that remained a prominent factor in my walk with God for the entire sixteen years that I lived there. I watched as the church grew from a couple thousand members to fifteen thousand or more members. The Pastor was gifted with an ability to teach the Word of God. His valuable teachings, with the assistance of the Holy Spirit, helped shape the woman I became in Christ. He taught me to forgive myself and receive the Lord's unending love and grace. I began to understand what a personal relationship with The Father, The Son, and The Holy Spirit is really all about. I realized that in order to truly enjoy the abundant life his Son came to give me, I had to forgive myself for all of the bad decisions I'd made, and for my role, not only in my own abortion, but in the premature deaths of hundreds of unborn babies.

Those three years were extremely difficult for me as I raised three children on my own in a city where there was no family to support me. My husband was locked away in a federal penitentiary, both physically and emotionally unavailable to me, but I felt the Lord walk beside me each and every day. His prominence in my life was palpable, a gift I would need more than once as I realized I was being prepared for more challenges that lay ahead.

It was during this time that I returned to school to study at the local community college. I had spent the majority of my teenage years and young adult life being conditioned, trained, and developed to work in the medical field. I was made to believe that I would grow up to work in medicine - a mechanic of the human body. But I found that when given the chance to chart my own path, I was much more fascinated with the human psyche than the human body. My passion was for counseling. My spiritual gifts as listed in Romans 12:8 were to show mercy, and do it cheerfully and to encourage others. The more I began to study topics surrounding social psychology and counseling the more I knew I'd finally found my calling in Christ.

After being incarcerated for only three years, my husband was released from prison in 1990. Instead of being deported, he was granted residency in the United States under a waiver neither one of us could understand, but I received the Lord's gifts gratefully. It was a time when we should have celebrated the opportunity for a fresh start – a new beginning for us both in Christ, but the enemy was waiting in the dark, ready to steal, kill, and destroy.

Upon my husband's release we committed to attending church together as a family and he agreed to be baptized after recommitting his life to Christ. We even enrolled together at the local community college where I began my studies in the arena of mental health and counseling, and he participated in an extensive English as a Second Language (ESL) program. Things were beginning to look up, but gradually he became focused on the need to provide for his family.

We fought the material desires and temptations that gravitated toward us, in hopes that somehow we could map another path to success. I continued to go to college, earning my Bachelor's degree in Social

Psychology, but my husband quickly became disillusioned with the hurdles that arose at every turn. Living in a border city plagued with drug cartels and readily available traffickers only made an "easy score" more tempting. He hoped to finally set us up for life.

Despite my husband's activities and acquaintances, I refused to abandon my walk with God and instead continued to focus on living righteously and moving forward in a field I believed with all my heart I was called to be a part of. I worked at a mental health clinic and obtained my license as a Substance Abuse Counselor. I volunteered hundreds of hours counseling at mental health wards, the local county jail, and worked with the homeless at nearby homeless shelters. I was attracted to those less fortunate then I (even as I refused to recognize the crisis within my own home). Yet, as a form of repentance, I continued to offer my heart to the Lord. I attended church regularly each week, committed to raising my children in a Christian environment. I also served my local community as a counselor to the broken. I even co-facilitated a ministry in my church that helped those battling addiction. It was a subject I was intimately familiar with as my husband had become an alcoholic.

In 1997, he reached his own rock bottom, as once again troubles with the law caught up to him and he was again incarcerated. Many of my friends and family felt that I'd served my penance and after fifteen years of marriage, I had every right to take the "high road" and walk away. But I believed in the sanctity of marriage and I wanted more than anything to honor God with my faith and commitment to the man I married. I believed that by standing firm beside a man who seemed beyond redemption, God would honor my act of faith with a miracle. I am humbled and grateful to relay that I was given my miracle.

After another long year by myself, waiting for my husband's release, I opted to pray and believe that things would change. And this time, after a year of being imprisoned my husband returned home, once again beaten and broken, but resolute to never return to illegal activity again.

Our marriage survived more in fifteen years than most couples will ever experience in a lifetime, but rather than allow the enemy the victory of what he intended for death, I stood on the Word of God and my husband and I became more united than ever.

I knew our time in El Paso was nearing its end, but I was blessed by the opportunity to pursue my Masters degree in Pastoral Counseling before preparing to move away. It was the final building block I needed to complete the good work the Lord was preparing for the next phase of my life.

In 2003, sixteen years after my arrival in El Paso, my husband and I began to make plans to return to our beloved city of Miami. My youngest child was nineteen -an adult- and we knew the time had come for us to return home. The wild lifestyles we'd once lived were long behind us. It was time to reconnect with family, including siblings my husband hadn't seen in over twenty years, and return to a city that embraced our cultural background. It was time to go home.

I didn't realize the significance of the pull on my heart to return to Miami. I didn't realize the purpose of God's plan in Hialeah. The wheels were in motion, and it was time for me to return home to put an end to what I'd once started. The Lord was granting me an opportunity to create a new legacy for the city I'd once exploited. It had been nearly twenty-five years of study, growth, and development. I had journeyed through turmoil and desolation. The Lord's hand cradled my broken heart and brought it healing. With the renewal of my mind and the healing of my heart it was time for my new journey in Christ, my divine purpose, to finally begin.

CHAPTER TEN

The Redemption Promise

From *Death* to **LIFE**

For all intents and purposes, the journey back to Miami was seamless, especially considering how long we'd been away. As everything quickly fell into place, I realized that my husband and I were being affirmed by the Lord as we followed the path he laid out for us. We'd raised three children, welcomed our first grandchild in 1995, a little girl, and survived separations that would have torn many other couples apart. Yet this was only the beginning of our newest chapter.

Upon arrival in Miami, we stayed with family before renting a beautiful condominium in the upscale suburb of Miami Lakes. I immediately found employment and began working at a local call center that assisted the elderly with their Medicare benefits. My husband also found work as a commercial driver for a local delivery company. The Lord continued to make a way for the provision in our lives so that we could begin our calling in Florida.

After a little less than twelve months in the area, I found myself taking a walk in our neighborhood and discovering the little church housed in the nearby schoolhouse. The following Sunday I began my new relationship with my new church home that would pave the way for my participation in bigger things.

After sixteen months of dedicated attendance the calling came as the visiting Reverend entered our service and placed my purpose directly in my lap.

I was not initially selected to work for the new pregnancy help clinic the Heartbeat of Miami team was establishing in the area, but I offered to serve as a volunteer anyway. There was no doubt in my mind that I had to do something, play any available role, walk through any door the Lord would open, in order to be a part of this incredible project.

I struggled with a guilty conscience from my participation in the start of the abortion wars on Miami's streets, but I continued to pray and seek repentance. The visiting Reverend was very interested in my story and wanted to use my testimony in marketing the new ministry. It was an exciting opportunity for me as I looked forward to the potential impact I could have on this sector of our community and the broken women I could counsel.

The project reached a turning point as I obeyed the whisper of the Holy Spirit and found myself driving back to the same busy corner where our original Women's Center was once located. I found myself plagued with flashbacks as I sat alone in my car. My mind turned toward a whirlwind of painful memories and buried torment that I'd spent nearly twenty-seven years running from, and had nearly successfully forgotten.

I wasn't sure why I was feeling pushed to return to this corner. I didn't know what to expect. What I did know was that the Reverend had requested I search for a building for the new facility and everything in my spirit was driving me toward the very same corner where it had all began.

I could almost hear the cries of the deceased babies as I approached the building. I knew this was Satan's conviction working overtime to try and convince me to turn away. I held strong as the building I once knew so well came closer and closer. I fought to push aside the tormenting cries of the helpless, the visions of pools of blood that came to the forefront of my mind. Gripping the steering wheel I began to pray. I asked Jesus to reveal his purpose and plan for this venture. I believed that my trip may have had its root in my own repentance. I'd been praying for forgiveness repeatedly, unwilling to fully accept that God could actually forgive me for something so tragic, something that so many years later was still causing devastation to the perfection and innocence of unborn lives. I wasn't sure what the Lord intended in bringing me back to where it began, but if it meant that I was to get on my knees and repent in the very place where the curse began, I was willing to do so. I was willing to do whatever it would take so that I might freely play a critical part in the growth of the new pregnancy life clinic.

When I finally arrived at the stop light I held my breath until the light turned green. I made a left turn into the parking lot of the physically unimposing building. It was a tiny structure, miniscule in comparison to today's large, modern medical facilities. Its exterior looked tired and worn. I stared at the front entrance of what once represented my biggest dreams and subsequent nightmares. It didn't seem so grand anymore. The building was just that - a building. Standing there helped to desensitize the power of the memories I'd held in my own psyche for so long. It was no longer the great and mighty building of memories past. It was just a building, one that appeared to be occupied by a local internist. I breathed a sigh of relief realizing, at a minimum, it was no longer an abortion facility.

I parked the car and stared at the very doors and windows I'd once known so well. I closed my eyes as I sat behind the driver's seat of my parked car and prayed for all that had happened behind the walls of that building, and for the strength and forgiveness I needed to receive in order to begin righting all the wrongs I'd committed. I asked for the Lord's divine ordination, asking him to place me on the front lines. In response I felt an acknowledgement within my spirit affirming that everything that had happened in my life up to that point would be to serve the purpose that would begin in this parking lot.

With my eyes closed tightly and my lips moving quickly in prayer I felt a tug in my spirit urging me to glance to my right. Obediently I turned my head and noticed an even smaller building housed in the same parking lot directly beside my mother's former medical center. It was a tiny building, but with some work it could be exactly what we were looking for.

A lump formed in my throat and tears sprang to my eyes as I stared at a sign in the corner of one of the front windows. I took a deep breath allowing the reality of what I was seeing really settle in. Housed in the exact same parking lot as our original abortion center, was a small building. The sign in the small window said, "*For Lease.*"

The Lord had led me to the place where we would establish the Heartbeat of Miami Pregnancy Help Clinic - a clinic that would save the lives of many unborn babies in the local community. I'd been brought to the place where he would place a clinic dedicated to life. Twenty-six years later I would return to the corner that was once covered with darkness and serve as a representative of Christ for those without a voice.

***

June 2007

Through the Lord's gentle leading and grace, I was hired to become the Clinical Director for the new Hialeah Pregnancy Help Clinic. In June of 2007 we had an open house dedication and moved in. Daily operations began only one month later on July 9th.

Every day that I drove to the small parking lot and unlocked the doors for operations I faced the goodness and grandeur of the Almighty for the work that he was doing in our very same community. I would press the buttons of the building's alarm, switch on the lights of each of the small, homelike decorated rooms and thank him for the glory that shone each and every day. We would welcome in his name the scared and confused women that nervously knocked on our doors each day, ready to show them his love and truth. This small clinic was mine to run. It was a gift of redemption given to me by Jesus not only to rectify the tragedies of my past but to relish the grace and mercy that he lovingly bestows upon his children. This was as much a gift of love for me, his child, as it was for the unborn babies safely growing in the wombs of their mothers.

Daily Operations

The idea behind the pregnancy help clinic was to assist mothers in bonding with their unborn babies. Our goal was to help educate these women about the stages of pregnancy and what truly constituted life. In doing so, we hoped that by sharing factual information about their pregnancy and alternative options to abortion, they would reconsider termination and would instead opt to choose life.

One of the greatest assets we had at our disposal was the sonogram machine and an ultrasound technician employed full time to operate it. The ultrasound was often the turning point in the decision process for a woman who had refused to acknowledge the fetus inside her as a separate, unique life. Day after day I witnessed firsthand and shared tears with women of all ages as they hesitantly turned their heads toward the monitor and watched the small baby inside of them move, almost playfully. The sounds of the strong rapid heartbeat of the tiny life inside them would fill the room with robust sounds of new life, immediately changing the circumstances for all involved. There was no denying the biological reality when faced with a screen that showed a small life, moving and growing inside of them.

It was a healing experience each and every time as I witnessed the hiccupping breaths and salty tears shed by remorseful mothers who had entered our facility only moments before, so certain of their decision to abort their pregnancy. When brought face to face with the reality of their unborn child, they could no longer fathom such an option. This was the power of the Almighty at work in our clinic, in my life, and in the lives of these women and their loved ones each and every day.

As I held their hands through the sonograms and our one-on-one counseling sessions, piece by piece my heart began to restore itself from the guilt and the condemnation of all the women I'd helped to do just the opposite so many years before. I cannot begin to think of a greater example of the goodness of God and the depth of his forgiveness, not only to forgive, but to allow such an opportunity for redemption.

Each and every day I tasted that forgiveness in the deepest part of my soul as I watched woman after woman enter our doors, more often than not thinking they were entering an abortion center. The look in their eyes was usually blank as they fought the emotions within their hearts. For a woman to willingly destroy the baby inside her goes against nature itself. To do so requires her, as a logical being, to fight the instincts inside her spirit that are screaming - this is wrong! What a gift it is to watch the Holy Spirit intervene and begin to crack the hardness of their hearts as we discuss their situations in a small counseling room decorated with a comfortable love seat and warmly glowing lamps. We provide a safe place to face the reality of the expectant mother's circumstances and her pending decisions. Often it's the first time she actually discusses the feasibility of actually having her baby. The breakthroughs begin to fill the small room and the glimmer of hope replaces the dullness in their eyes. This is when I witness firsthand the first stages of healing as these women begin to choose life. It's usually the first time since the shock of discovering they were pregnant that things finally begin to feel right within them.

The beauty of our day-to-day happenings is the miracles of God's influence in the lives of some of our women. We see young women who are somewhat undecided about their situations and easy to convince. But some of our cases are clearly-drawn battles with demonic forces directly from the darkness of Hell. Allow me to share a few examples to help highlight the impact of what the Lord began to do in our small community of Hialeah, Florida.

The Immigrant

On one sunny afternoon a tall dark haired women walked through the doors of our clinic. She was stunningly beautiful but I could see the sorrow in her expression. Her body language made it clear that she was nervous about entering our facility. Experience had taught me to tread very carefully when counseling someone who was clearly very guarded and private.

As I took down her information and escorted her into our counseling room she was fidgety and nervous. She kept staring at the door I gently closed as though she was expecting someone to burst in. Looking at her further, I noticed that her hands were trembling. I encouraged her to take a deep breath and relax, as she had entered a safe place. She peppered me with questions about the privacy acts and what exactly we were bound to keep private between us. I assured her that with the provisions of the Health Insurance Portability and Accountability Act (HIPAA) she could feel safe to disclose personal information without fear of retribution.

She finally took the deep breath I'd suggested and closed her eyes as she began to explain her situation. She was living in the United States as an illegal immigrant. She had escaped her home country in the Caribbean, leaving behind two daughters, in order to establish a better life for them in the US. Leaving her children had been a devastatingly difficult decision but she was determined to find success in the "land of plenty" and eventually obtain her papers and send for her children. Sadly she allowed herself to become very involved with a troubled man she met in Miami and had recently discovered she was pregnant.

Having the baby did not seem possible to her. It went against everything she was trying to do for herself and her children. As I listened to her story my mind went back to the hundreds of female Cuban immigrants I'd spoken to so many years before in the very same circumstances, only then I was convincing them to abort their babies. This time, I had to help convince her to choose life.

She continued to share with me that she had already been to the abortion facility and was gowned and on the operating table awaiting a doctor who was running late. As she lay on that table anxious to get the procedure over with, the reality of what she was doing began to weigh heavily on her chest. When the doctor finally did arrive she jumped off the table grabbed her balled up clothing and ran to her car, unable to go through with her original decision.

As this beautiful but distraught woman sat in front of me in tears, I reached for her hand and allowed her a moment of silence to collect her thoughts. Praying internally for wisdom I allowed the Holy Spirit to speak through me as I softly whispered, "It's OK, you can have your baby."

Immediately I saw a light spark in her eyes as she accepted my words. It was the reassurance, the affirmation of her own spirit that she needed, and immediately her decision seemed so clear. I'm so proud to be able to say that eight months later she delivered a beautiful baby girl and is now legally residing in the United States continuing her journey toward success.

The Culture Factor

One of the greatest challenges I faced as a new pregnancy help counselor was the cultural opposition posed by a young woman from India.

I had been contacted by a local pro-life OB/GYN who had been treating this young woman for infertility. She was staying in Miami temporarily as a cancer researcher at the University of Miami, while her husband, her seven year old daughter, and her parents continued to reside in India. Her husband visited her frequently, but after several years of trying to have another child she was distraught because she had been unable to conceive. The couple reached out to a fertility specialist for help getting pregnant. By the grace of God, she and her husband were finally able to conceive and she was approximately thirteen weeks pregnant when her OB/GYN contacted me. The doctor was concerned because the woman revealed that since their first child was a daughter; their second child had to be a son in order to carry on the family name. This was critical in the Indian culture. In addition, her own parents had only had two girls, she and her sister, which made her father adamantly opposed to her also carrying to term another girl. Much to her dismay, she revealed to her doctor that if the baby was discovered to be a girl they would be forced to terminate the pregnancy, even though the pregnancy was itself a miracle.

I asked the doctor to refer her to our clinic for counseling and she came to see me right away. We discussed the cultural pressure to abort a baby girl, and she was adamant that there were no alternatives to termination if the baby was indeed a girl. I asked her to pray with me and because she was a Muslim, we agreed to pray to the Father of Isaac, Abraham, and Jacob for intervention and assistance. I was also able to convince her to wait until we could determine the sex of the baby before making any decisions related to termination. I could tell that she was becoming very attached to her unborn baby and needed a reason to postpone termination, so she readily agreed to wait.

Two instances passed where we did the sonogram and were unable to determine the sex, but in her heart the young women felt that her baby was, in fact, a little girl. I managed to convince her to wait one more week and finally on the third try, her suspicions were confirmed - her baby was a baby girl.

The tension in the ultrasound room was palpable as we delivered the news. It pained me to see the tragedy on this young woman's face. She had obviously already bonded with her baby and did not want to have an abortion. But the duty to her culture was very strong and it left her feeling as though she had no other choice.

Immediately after she left our clinic that afternoon, the ultrasound technician and I got down on bended knee and began to pray for the life of the baby. After three ultrasounds we'd also become attached to the little life within this woman's womb. We placed its life in the Father's hands and asked for a miracle. Thankfully, a miracle was exactly what we were given. One week later, the young woman called to tell us that her husband and father had both had a change of heart and would permit her to carry her pregnancy to term, despite the child's gender. It was a joyous revelation for us all as we raised our eyes toward Heaven and thanked the Lord for his goodness.

The Building

Nearly each and every day there was a story of miracles in my building. I was awe-inspired on a daily basis by the immensity and passion of God's love. I had returned to the same location of my greatest sins to redeem myself and do the greatest work for the Kingdom of Heaven that I'd ever done in my life. Each and every day I felt myself armed with the armor of God as I entered the battlefield for the lives of the unborn. It was inspiring as I stared out the window of our clinic and looked at the building next door, the very building that had once brought so much death and destruction to the people of this city. That building housed a diagnostic center and clinic for internal medicine, but still brought me such vivid memories of the ugliness and destruction behind Satan's attacks on the human race.

The war became clearer as I witnessed firsthand the viciousness behind the targeting of the most innocent of God's creation - the voiceless. These tiny souls, so innocent, are fully dependant on the choice made by their mothers in order to survive. It made me angry to think of the kind of hate that spawned this type of attack, but it also fueled my motivation to continue to fight for the right of the unborn to live.

Staring at that building next door reminded me of the divine and unique purpose the Lord had bestowed on me and reaffirmed my dedication to continue to see it through. Yet I did not realize that the opening of this clinic was not the final chapter of this story. The Lord has plans to conquer the enemy and win the battle at a level beyond our greatest expectations. What happened next was more inspiring then anything I'd seen yet.

Conquered

CHAPTER ELEVEN

It All Comes Full Circle
MORE THAN CONQUERORS

You intended to harm me, but God intended it all for good. He brought me to this position so I could save the lives of many people. – Genesis 50:20
(New Living Translation)

In September 2012 a faith-filled couple entered our clinic, obediently following the call of the Holy Spirit in their lives. They were well known for their missionary work and the ministry they led as part of a very large church in the area. Neither one of us knew exactly what God's purpose was for their visit, but we sat down together in the counseling room and I began to share my story and the vision of our ministry in the saving of unborn lives. I felt a pressing in my spirit to discuss the need to expand our facility and provide services to more woman than ever before. I told them about the abortion rates in Miami Dade County and the impact abortion centers were having in the lives of thousands of women in our own community. I fought back tears of determination and sorrow as I remembered the sad faces that entered our clinic every day back in the 1970's determined to find freedom through abortion.

The couple quietly listened as I shared my vision of one day "taking back the land" as the Lord said Israel would do in Jeremiah 49:2 *In the days to come," says the LORD, "I will sound the battle cry against your city of*

Rabbah. It will become a desolate heap of ruins, and the neighboring towns will be burned. Then Israel will take back the land you took from her," says the LORD.

I believed that there was a need to expand our facility and I believed with all my heart that the building next to ours, the original building I'd once occupied, would be the answer to that expansion.

We held hands and bowed our heads in prayer, expecting a miracle at the hand of our Heavenly Father. As we prayed my soul felt refreshed. As I escorted the couple to the door to bid them farewell, I was filled with energy at the endless possibilities available when partnering with Jesus and his love for his children.

Shortly after their departure the telephone rang. I had no reason to think this call would concern anything beyond the normal day-to-day happenings of the clinic, but I was wrong. It was my landlord, the owner of both our current building and the building next door. She informed me that the current tenants next door had decided to relocate their clinic elsewhere and the building would soon be available for rent, if we were interested.

My hands shook with the miracle of what I was hearing. I thanked him for the call and hung up the phone. I felt like I was moving in slow motion underwater, but I silently made my way to the small room that faced the building next door and got down on bended knee. I lowered my forehead to the cold tiles in reverence to the Almighty as I prayed for my biggest dream to come to fruition. I prayed that he would grace me with mercy and allow me the full redemption of reclaiming the building that once represented death, using it instead to fight the good fight for life. Most of all, I thanked him for his unrestricted forgiveness and willingness to choose me to represent this ministry in Miami.

In one fateful morning I felt as though everything had changed for the better. But the enemy was still there; the battle for the building had only begun.

I contacted the president of our organization about the possibility of moving into the building next door and expanding our facility. She was initially very concerned with the additional rental costs and the money needed to renovate the building. Based on all of the costs associated with the project, it just didn't appear to be financially feasible.

I was devastated, but didn't allow my emotions to get the best of me. I knew the timing was no coincidence. I knew that the Lord had a specific purpose for our ministry and for the building next door, and I knew that I needed to continue to pray without ceasing and believe in a miracle.

Months ticked by as I drove into our shared parking lot each and every morning and prayed for the redemption project. There didn't appear to be any interest in the building and each month that it remained vacant I held on to my hope that the Lord would deliver this building into our hands.

In December of 2012, three months after the building became available; the evidence of things unseen came to fruition. The original couple I'd prayed with in September, and an army of twenty of the Lord's followers, showed up at our facility. They were volunteers all working in the same ministry. They walked through the vacant building. As if in fulfillment of a prophesy, the building's owner gave me the keys to the building, In case we were ready to lease it. . I escorted the group through the halls of the very structure I'd once known so well, and quietly prayed. I watched as they looked around and walked through each of the rooms until they all finally returned to the empty lobby.

To the glory of God they discussed it among themselves and let me know that they were in agreement. This was a project they wanted to take on as a mission for their ministry. All we had to do was rent the facility and they would provide all of the necessary labor and materials for renovations. Amazingly, the expenses associated with renovating the facility were eliminated at that very moment.

The following month, the landlord agreed to a lease with the Heartbeat of Miami Ministries at a reduced price from what he had been receiving from the prior tenants. All of the financial concerns associated with the move were eliminated. The president of Heartbeat of Miami Ministries and I could see the hand of God moving in order to make our vision a reality.

Armed with a team of volunteers and a newly signed lease, I entered the doors of the building whose walls had once witnessed the death and destruction of thousands of innocent babies. Standing in the center of the lobby I closed my eyes and allowed my memories to take me back nearly thirty-five years where I once stood as a young girl, only twenty years old. I remembered the black and white linoleum tiled floors, the large red soda fountain-styled couch, the empty stares of the women, shamed, waiting their turn for the slaughter.

I allowed the tears to course down my cheeks as I relived that Sunday morning when *I* was the patient, when it was *my* turn to be escorted in a backless hospital gown to the sterile white hospital bed where my feet were placed in the cold metal stirrups. I allowed myself to mourn the child, who I believed to be my son, the boy I gave up that fateful morning. But I also allowed my tears to flow from the joy of current possibilities. I took solace in the goodness of God allowing me a chance to redeem my wicked ways. I was now being offered a chance to participate in saving the lives of thousands of babies within the very same walls. My hopes were to save at least five unborn lives for every one life that had been destroyed here before. This would be the great victory in the city of Miami - the crusade for the innocent. And this building would be in the forefront of the battle. Our ministry was moving toward another level, and I could only be grateful that I was allowed a chance to be a part of it all.

It was time to wage war on the forces of evil and save the women and their loved ones who would walk through our doors convinced of the lies being whispered into their hearts. . This was a new opportunity, a new hope for their lives, and I would continue to fight with everything I had for the rights of their children. It was no coincidence that I'd been brought back to this place after so many years away. The even greater story was our purpose in our new facility.

Healing for Many

Renovations of the new building began immediately. Crews of volunteers from the church showed up motivated and excited to participate in the Lord's local victory. I was awestruck by the first two men who walked through the door; they introduced themselves to me, and both of them were named Michael. Their name was significant as it was the name I'd given to the child I'd aborted in that very building. As I stood there and shook hands with these two individuals that would help restore our building, I was touched by the significance of their names and felt that it may have been a sign from Heaven that my unborn son was watching me from above in approval of what we were doing here.

The second miracle that shortly followed was presented to me by a lovely young woman. She was the wife of one of our volunteers. Her husband had approached me during some of the cleanup work we were doing. He mentioned that his wife was still grieving over an abortion she'd suffered while involved in a previous relationship. He was hoping to invite her to participate in the mission of renovating the building in the hope that it might help her heal from her own loss. I encouraged him to welcome her on board and looked forward to inviting her to participate in our next Post Abortive Healing class.

As an employee and co-founder of the Heartbeat of Miami Pregnancy Help Clinic I have led a nine week Post Abortive Healing class twice a year designed especially to help women work through the emotional stress associated with abortion. Our program is derived from a Bible study written and developed by Linda Cochrane entitled *Forgiven and Set Free.* The intent behind this study is to guide those who are suffering to bring their emotional scars from abortion "out of the dark past and into his holy light," where true and lasting healing can take place. As I listened to the concerns of the local volunteer for his wife, I felt that she might be a prime candidate to participate in the first post-abortive class to take place in our new building.

Shortly after our initial meeting his wife showed up to help volunteer. Much to my surprise, the woman stood trembling at the door. Her hand covered her mouth in shock, and she began to cry.

I immediately recognized her reaction. I'd had a similar experience upon first entering the building after so many years as well. In fact, I think through the Holy Spirit's wisdom I was immediately enlightened about her trouble. I approached her quietly and wrapped my arms around her in a warm embrace allowing her to cry into my shoulder as she affirmed that this was the building where she'd had the abortion that still haunted her so many years later. I believed her situation was a preview or revelation of the healing power that would be evident in our new center. Not only did we have our first post-abortive candidate before the center even opened its doors, but the similarity that both she and I, involved in the restoration of a center that once served as the center of death for our unborn babies would now be placed together in her healing - spoke volumes. We decided to name the next Post Abortive Bible Study, "Restoring the Heart," and I looked forward to the group of women who'd be working toward their own healing.

Shortly after, a second woman came forward during the renovation process. She, too, was surprised to discover that ours was the very same building where she'd suffered multiple abortions. After sharing her story I invited her to participate in the *Restoring the Heart* group later that year.

I sat amazed at the truth that all three of us shared such an unusual commonality, but marveled at the message the Lord was bestowing on us about the promise related to the building.

Just as I thought we would be prepared to move forward in managing the logistics of our healing session, I discovered that my co-facilitator, the fourth member of our launch group, had also had an abortion in that very building! What an amazing testimony it was for each of us, and now for me, to share with the world, the perfection of God's plan and design.

Carefully he crafted an opportunity for four women to come together and truly receive spiritual healing within the very same walls where it all began for each of us. We would launch the mission of our clinic, not only to save the lives of the unborn in the present community, but to heal the hearts and souls of the women from its past. It was an area of ministry I hadn't even considered up until then.

Praise be to Jesus!

The Grand Opening to Present Day

Three months after signing the new lease the clinic opened its doors to the public and began operations. It was April 30, 2013 only one month shy of thirty-five years from the opening of its operations as an abortion center. For those of us who had once suffered within its doors, those thirty-five years felt more like thirty-five days.

The memories of the tragedies that occurred within those walls were still very fresh in my mind, but I used their vividness for good rather than for torment. No longer would I allow my memories to serve as a noose around my throat, wrapped with guilt and condemnation. Instead those memories served as reminder of our victory in Christ. Those memories are what drive me, on a daily basis, to speak truth and light to the hundreds of women that enter our doors day in and day out. I am resolved that each and every day that I am graced with the Lord's purpose in this center, I will dedicate my efforts to healing the women who've been mauled physically and spiritually by abortion. I vow to do everything in my power to prevent the deaths of any more innocent children that enter our doors within the wombs of their mothers.

In July of this year we launched our first Post-Abortive Counseling group at our new clinic. The four of us were deeply touched, and experienced a great healing as we realized the ability of our Heavenly Father's unfailing love and forgiveness to take what was destined for evil and turn it into good. Through the transformation of our building we witnessed the tangible changes that mirrored the intended changes within each and every one of us. I watched as they restored their hearts and received forgiveness for the tragedy of their abortions. They named our unborn children and gave them an earthly identity, unwilling to allow our grief to be forbidden any longer. As we embraced the new chapter and renewal within our building we embraced the newness of the spirit within our bodies. The chains of guilt were broken and we were finally set free.

I've spent six months in our new building and shared my story and my history in our location with many who've walked through our doors, but I knew that it was time to put my story to print. I wanted to touch the lives of many who may never actually set foot in our facility but may need to hear the promise of redemption that is represented by my personal journey in the industry of abortion and of now saving lives. So many broken hearts reside in our world, walking through empty and hollow lives each day, unwilling to believe that there is a God who is willing to forgive them for their transgressions.

I was once that person. I felt that my sins were too grave, that I could never dare to ask for forgiveness. But I was wrong; I was very, very wrong. Not only was I forgiven, but I was offered an opportunity at redemption greater than I could have ever imagined. Now, as I drive down the familiar street in the heart of Hialeah to the building on the corner, I drive with great pride at what that building represents in our community. What was once intended for death has become a center for life. What was once surrounded in darkness now shines as a light for all to see. What was once a building designed for destruction has become a source of solace and healing for the broken. I serve a mighty and glorious Lord; a Heavenly Father who has called me to be more than a conqueror, who has shown me through his fierce love for the innocent the victory of having won the battle for life.

This experience has defined my life's purpose and existence, and now I share my story for all to discover the power of redemption. The very same kind of redemption can be available for each and everyone on this earth who wants it. All we have to do is ask. I hope that after reading this you are inspired to begin your own journey as a conqueror. I pray that the grace of God be with you always. Amen.

Conquered

EPILOGUE

The Statistics
The Fight for Life

What began with one small clinic in the small suburb of Hialeah has now expanded into two clinics, with the possibility of expanding into a third. The growth of our organization is a testament to the needs of the community for the truth about pregnancy and the life that resides within a pregnant woman's womb.

Heartbeat of Miami Pregnancy Help Clinic sees hundreds of women each and every week. We provide free pregnancy tests, pregnancy counseling, and ultrasounds. We help to give women an opportunity to freely express their concerns about their pregnancy, but also the chance to learn that the bond between mother and child is undeniable. Often times the majority of the women and couples we see simply need to hear someone vocalize that having their baby is a very distinct and realistic possibility. Since the 2007 launch of the Heartbeat of Miami Pregnancy Help Clinics, providing something as simple as education for our patrons has saved the lives of thousands of babies.

Our mission is to open three to five life-changing pregnancy resource centers in the neediest neighborhoods of Miami over the next two years. Our goal is to help stop the genocide of the unborn in our community. In Miami, this war is primarily affecting the minority populations in the area. We believe that with the support of local volunteers generously providing their time and support, and the generous donations of those whose compassion encompasses the cause, we can continue to fight for the voiceless and win more and more of the spiritual battles taking place for these tiny souls.

If you are interested in learning more about the Heartbeat of Miami Pregnancy Help Clinic, please feel free to contact us at:

Heartbeat of Miami
301 Westward Drive
Miami Springs, FL 33166
1 (888) 981-7770
www.heartbeatofmiami.org

I've had the honor and privilege of working with a wonderful group of people for an amazing cause for nearly seven years. It is a gift directly from the Lord that I serve on this earth, knowing that I am walking in my own divine purpose - the saving of many lives. However, I can't end my story without mentioning the importance and personal impact of a very special service we offer for the hurting. And that is post-- abortive counseling.

It's been a gift in my life to witness the healing of broken hearts as we meet over a nine week bible study with women who've struggled and are currently struggling after terminating a pregnancy. Post abortive stress is very real, but there is help and it begins with spiritual healing. Heartbeat of Miami Pregnancy Help Clinics aren't only saving the lives of the unborn, but the broken spirits of the women who once chose to end those lives, and now need the kind of healing that can only be found through the love, mercy and grace of Jesus Christ. Our bible study helps them walk through each stage of grief and affliction, and offers Biblical truth and healing for its participants.

Whether it's through pregnancy crisis counseling or post-abortive healing, our organization has services to help heal and provide the truth, beauty, and power of the Gospel. I hope that by reading this book you have become enlightened to the healing power of God and the capacity he has for forgiveness.

I once stood on the front lines of the dark army. I helped escort hundreds of women into a room where their greatest nightmares were only just beginning. I participated in the shedding of innocent blood and the taking of innocent lives. Yet not even that was enough to cause our merciful Creator to turn away from me. Instead he healed my heart, renewed my mind and transformed me from the inside out. Now I can proudly say that I boldly fight for the Kingdom of Heaven. I am once again on the front lines, but this time I carry the sword of the spirit as I challenge the forces of darkness in the daily battle for innocent lives. Based on the growth we are seeing in our organization in Miami and within the walls of our new building, it is apparent that the victory is ours and the battle will be won!

Conquered

ACKNOWLEDGMENTS

As always I must first thank my Heavenly Father for his divine love, wisdom, and purpose in my life. Without my Lord, life is meaningless. I'm also deeply grateful to Jeanne Pernia and Irene Liberman, the two women I proudly call my mother and my grandmother. Without them there would not be a story. It was their first hand accounts and willingness to share the candid and tragic truth that allowed me to translate their emotions and their experience into words. Sharing the truth of such harsh memories isn't always the easiest thing to do, but their courage has allowed me to capture a piece of our family legacy. I must also thank Mary Salter for her tireless editing efforts and ensuring that the final version was perfect. And Martha Avila, President and Co-founder of the Heartbeat of Miami Ministries, for her endless support and passion for the project. And as always, I am most deeply thankful to my husband, Alberto, for his inspiration, support, and so very much more.

SOURCES

INTERVIEWS

Jeanne Pernia and Irene Liberman

WORKS CITED

"Answering the Call." *About* Us. 2007-2010. Heartbeat of Miami. 1 August 2013.<http://www.heartbeatof miami.org/about/>

"D and C (Dilation and Curettage)." *Women's Health.* 5 August 2012. WebMD. 4 August 2013. <http://women.webmd.com/guide/d-and-c-dilation-and-curettage>

"Data and Statistics." *Reproductive Health.* 11 April 2013. Centers for Disease Control and Prevention. 1 August 2013. < http://www.cdc.gov/reproductive health/Data_Stats/>

"Demographics." *Hialeah, Florida.* 4 October 2013. Wikipedia. 4 August 2013. <http://en.wikipedia.org/ wiki/Hialeah,_Florida>

"Facts About Mifepristone (RU-486)."*Abortion Facts.*
31 January 2008. National Abortion Federation. 4
August 2013. <http://www.prochoice.org/about_
abortion/facts/facts_mifepristone.html>

"Facts and Figures Relating to the Frequency of
Abortion in the United States." *U.S. Abortion
Statistics.* 21 June 2013. Abort73.com. 1 August
2013.< http://www.abort73.com/abortion_facts/us_
abortion_statistics/>

"Hialeah History Chronology." *Hialeah.* 16 October
2012. Florida Community Studies Consortium. 4
August 2013. <http://floridacommunitystudies.org/
csc/book/export/html/169>

"History of Hialeah." *About Hialeah.* 2012. City of
Hialeah. 4 August 2013. <http://www.hialeahfl.gov/
index.php?option=com_content&view=article&id=11
&Itemid=207&lang=en>

Kumar, Prashant. "Thiopentone Sodium." May 2012.
Anaesthesiology and Critical Care. 5 August 2013.
<http://anaesthesia.co.in/wp-content/uploads/
2012/05/Thiopentone-Sodium1.pdf>

"Miami-Dade County Florida." *State and County Quick
Facts.* 27 June 2013 .United States Census Bureau. 1
August 2013. <http://quickfacts.census.gov/qfd/states
/12/12086.html>

"Promoting and Supporting the Development of
   Pregnancy Centers in Underserved Communities."
   Underserved Outreach. 1 August 2013. CareNet.
   2013. <https://www.care-net.org/ourwork/program
   .php?id=1>

"State Facts About Abortion: Florida." *State Center.*
   2013. The Guttmacher Institute. 1 August 2013.
   <http://www.guttmacher.org/pubs/sfaa/florida.html>

"The History of Operation of Pedro Pan." *History.* 2009.
   Operation Pedro Pan Group, Inc. 4 August 2013.
   < http://www.pedropan.org/category/history>

33674327R00081

Made in the USA
Charleston, SC
21 September 2014